WOMEN OF SPIRIT

Women of Spirit

Volume One

Compiled and photographed by

Susie Mackie

SilverWood

First edition published in 2018 by SilverWood Books
Revised second edition 2023

SilverWood Books Ltd
14 Small Street, Bristol, BS1 1DE, United Kingdom

www.silverwoodbooks.co.uk

Copyright © Susie Mackie 2023

The right of Susie Mackie to be identified as the author
of this work has been asserted in accordance with the
Copyright, Designs and Patents Act 1988 Sections 77 and 78.

All rights reserved. No part of this publication may be reproduced,
stored in a retrieval system, or transmitted in any form or by any means,
electronic, mechanical, photocopying, recording or otherwise, without
prior permission of the copyright holder.

ISBN 978-1-80042-274-2 (paperback)
Also available as an ebook

British Library Cataloguing in Publication Data
A CIP catalogue record for this book is available from the British Library

Page design and typesetting by SilverWood Books

*To my own two beautiful, spirited, daughters, Lottie and Bea,
and to my dear friend Sally, whose story was to be featured in this book,
but who is gone too soon.*

Contents

	Acknowledgements	9
	Foreword by Jo Parfitt	11
One	**The Road to Self-Love**	
	Carol May	16
	Helen Courtney	24
	Sam Geddes	38
	Susie Mackie	50
	Lacey Thompson	60
	Judi Burke	68
	Jenna Harwin	76
	Gabriella Guglielminotti Trivel	84
	Dawn Swinley	96
Two	**Failure is Not an Option**	
	Sejal Payne	104
	Chris Ramsbottom	112
	Jo Parfitt	120
	Helen Dickson	126
Three	**Perfect in My Imperfections**	
	Victoria Petkovic-Short	138
	Mary Lunnen	146
	Kate Beddow	156
	Louisa	168
	Laura Steckler	179
Four	**Death Does Not Define Me**	
	Rachel Singers	190
	Sam Bawden	198
	Sue Williams	208

Di Lofting	222
Alice and Lucy Steels	228
Author's Note	235
Mission Statement	237

Acknowledgements

With heartfelt thanks to my parents and daughters for all your love and support over the years, you are just amazing and I love you beyond words.

Carie Lyndene, your unwavering belief in me and your brilliant business mentoring over the past three years has, as I knew it would, changed my life. Thank you.

Cheltenham, you have embraced me and provided so many fabulous friends who have given their love, support, laughter, and a listening ear way beyond the call of duty. After only three years I feel you are my home.

I mustn't forget the corner shop, which has provided regular and very necessary supplies of Merlot and dark chocolate whenever needed.

And to all the incredible, spirited women whose stories grace the pages of this book – without you it would of course not exist. You are a joy and an inspiration and I am blessed with our blossoming friendships.

Foreword

To be invited to write the foreword to this wonderful book is both an honour and a humbling experience. It is an honour, because this is a unique publication that shows the author/photographer's immense talent alongside those of its featured women. And it is an honour because I too have been chosen to join the collection. Yet I am humbled. It is hard to consider myself worthy to have my face shown alongside women whose spirit appears so much greater than my own, the author's included.

In the following pages Susie shows us that the connection between 'spirit' and 'inspiration' goes beyond the fact that they both derive from the same root, the Latin verb *inspirare*, meaning to breathe or blow into. The photography and prose shown here breathes life into the personalities of these remarkable women.

The women featured here have all dug deep and found ways to rise up and away from times of despair. Here we see how women beat illness, disempowerment, racism, bereavement and lack of acceptance. The challenges faced here are commonplace, the way these women of spirit conquered them is exemplary.

Susie's own spirited nature is epitomised by this, her first, brave work, achieved as she herself battled long term illness, marriage breakdown and financial difficulties. It stands as testament to her own unbreakable spirit that she never once questioned her ability to write, yet she had never written anything before. She never once doubted her ability to source the women featured here, nor to persuade them to be included in the project. She never considered that her photographs would be anything less than perfect for publication, nor that her book may have been without that necessary 'wow factor'. Doubts such as these are what sabotage the potential success craved by 'other people'. These women are not 'other people'. These women of spirit could never have afforded to believe they might fail. For when the chips are down we know that the only person we can count on is our self. Were that one person to have no faith in us either, then what hope would remain? Self-doubt crushes the spirit like an old newspaper, screws it into a little ball and tosses it aside.

Collectively, myself included, the drive, passion and determination of these women has had much to do with their success. But more than these it is clear that without an indomitable spirit and self-belief as their allies, there would be no *Women of Spirit*.

Jo Parfitt – www.summertimepublishing.com

WOMEN OF SPIRIT

One

The Road to Self-Love

A new life begins for us with every second.
Let us go forward joyously to meet it.
We must press on, whether we will or no,
and we shall walk better with our eyes before us
Than with them ever cast behind.

Jerome K. Jerome (1859 – 1927)

Carol May

Warmth and wisdom ooze from this woman. She is a beautiful example of how to turn your life around, to use your painful experiences in order to grow, and ultimately help others. No longer a 'people pleaser,' she has finally found a way to make healthy choices for both mind and body, which are absolutely connected, and to nurture others through her profession as a weight loss counsellor and eating disorders therapist.

I WAS BORN FOUR YEARS AGO, at the physical age of fifty-nine. My birth was traumatic, full of pain and tears, and it took six months of working with one of the most amazing women I have ever met to reach this point. Finding my real 'self' for the first time in my life was life changing.

I'm a child of the 1950's and grew up as a 'people pleaser' and a nurturer, learning to set aside and eventually cover up my feelings and my dreams. I decided I was not of value, not worthy of being seen or heard – not because my parents were bad or because they didn't love me but because childhood is the time when we create faulty thinking and faulty beliefs as a result of unconscious decisions we make – and these can go on to shape our whole life and trajectory.

By the age of twelve I had developed a very poor body image and an unhealthy relationship with carbohydrates and sugary foods; my body disgusted me, and I hated it. The family doctor put me on a diet and the same appetite suppressant, amphetamines, which he gave my mum. It seems crazy now in light of our current knowledge about what dieting and amphetamines do to our bodies, but this was the 1960's when the use of appetite suppressants for weight loss was considered 'cutting edge.'

And so began almost fifty years of yoyo dieting, not a recognised eating disorder but most certainly disordered eating! I would binge eat and then almost starve myself, and congratulate myself for having enough willpower to lose some weight. I would eat normally in public then raid the fridge when I was on my own, finishing off all the leftovers in one go so I could go back to 'being good' tomorrow. I lived a life obsessed with my body, food, and the number on the scales every morning which dictated my mood that day. I had joined the rollercoaster of emotional eating and yoyo dieting. I was enslaved by this obsession and I felt as though there was no way out. I became adept at hiding from the camera, and in group shots, being tall, I hid at the back. I also experienced severe anxiety and panic attacks as a teenager, something which continued into adulthood. My pain became a deep black hole which I smothered with food; I slowly lost sight of the real me. I now know that we cannot disconnect from pain and distress without disconnecting from joy, love and happiness as well, but back then I had no idea what was happening and in fact for a long time I thought that maybe this was how everyone felt.

My husband and I met when I was just seventeen, and we dated for almost three years before we broke up because I didn't want to get married. I was a student by then with big dreams and marriage was the last thing on my mind. However, once I graduated, I experienced the old fear and anxiety again, and so I went back to him; I went back to safety and familiarity.

However, that 'safety' was far from safe as it turned out – we had a dysfunctional and co-dependent relationship which was doomed from the start. He made fun of me in public even though I repeatedly asked him not to; he criticised my ambitions, and never ever said he was proud of my achievements, even when I had a book published. I hadn't realised how much this hurt until the new man in my life said how proud he was of me and I burst into tears.

Two difficult pregnancies and traumatic births by emergency Caesarean section left me with a saggy belly and damaged muscles, vertical and horizontal scars and the inevitable silvery stretchmarks everywhere. When I looked in the mirror, instead of seeing a miraculous body which had survived AND produced two beautiful children, I just felt disgust. Add chronic low self-esteem and severe post-natal depression into the mix plus anxiety and stress, it was no wonder my inner critical voice was on overdrive telling me I was useless, weak, stupid, lazy, greedy and worthless with no willpower.

And so, the pattern of my life was set, with medication becoming my long-term crutch. On the surface, I would appear happy but underneath it I was battling chronic poor mental health, disordered eating bordering on an eating disorder, a deep sense of worthlessness I can't even begin to describe, and a feeling of numbness I just assumed was normal. However, I had a sense that there was more to life than this and I found myself beginning to search – although I had no idea what I was searching for, I just knew there had to be more to life than what I was experiencing.

At the age of forty I went into 'therapy' for the first time and began my healing journey, a journey which continues to this day. I don't believe we ever stop learning about ourselves and our place in the world. But it was the beginning of my awakening to the power of the mind and our ability to change our reality, if we choose.

And then the perimenopause kicked in, which no one had warned me about. My hair fell out in lumps, my body shape changed seemingly overnight, my weight rocketed up yet again and my emotional fuse was so short that if you blinked you missed the upbeat moments. Each hot flush brought on a panic attack and the depression deepened. Oh, I could wear a mask of conviviality long enough to convince most people that I was 'fine', but behind all this I turned to extreme dieting to try and finally lose the excess weight. But the weight bounced back on as I went back to normal food.

So, I decided to train as a Weight Loss Counsellor and Eating Disorders Therapist and began the next phase of my healing journey… the part where I learned just how much damage I had done to my body, that dieting doesn't work and why, and that food is not actually the issue here. I learned what was in my black hole and how to heal it, why I ate emotionally and how to use the tools I was learning in order to change. Suddenly, the jigsaw pieces of my life started fitting together and as I began to heal, I found I absolutely loved working with other women to help them heal too, and that I was actually good at what I did! For the first time in my life I won a prize. I was proud of myself. But as I was on the way up, my husband was on a downward spiral into depression and alcoholism, partly due to chronic stress about money (he was a tenant farmer) and on Christmas Day 2008 he walked away…and I fell apart again.

When I think back I can see why I went back to him in my twenties, why I craved security and why I feared the unfamiliar, even though it's what I craved in my heart. And why these fears were the reason I stayed with him when he became an aggressive and nasty alcoholic. Seems stupid now, knowing all I now know and having broken free of the patterning.

There followed a long period of severe stress and deep depression, adrenal fatigue, bankruptcy, and eighteen months of homelessness – although thankfully I was never actually on the streets.

Looking back, they were very dark times indeed, and at one point I did consider checking out, for the second time in my life. But my daughter talked me round and for that I will always be grateful.

So, how did I get through it?

Initially, with sheer bloody mindedness and determination; I was not going to be beaten! I researched adrenal fatigue, followed the programme I found and got better. It wasn't easy, but I knew I had no other choice. Now I use what I learned to help other women.

I actively engaged in a collaborative form of counselling which was offered to me by my doctor and I was fortunate to see her weekly for eight months. With her help, I was able to dig deep and do the work necessary to come off most of the medication at last.

But life was still hard, money was very short, and in addition, I was bullied at work; I was still on an emotional rollercoaster fuelled by anger, disappointment in myself and others; and a deep, deep hurt.

Then Wendy, an amazing woman with whom I had previously done some healing work, contacted me and my six-month journey with her began, from pain to my rebirth. I know that might sound over dramatic, but it is the only way I can describe how it felt to finally release forever the years of depression, pain, stress, and anger, and to finally learn how it physically felt to really feel feelings and emotions, to experience real happiness and joy every day whatever was happening in my life; for the first time I was actually waking up full of energy and enthusiasm. I finally learned what love felt like in my body rather than to just have a 'knowing' in my head.

I began learning about the power of respecting and honouring the body I lived in, how to be compassionate and accepting towards myself and to stop comparing myself to others. I learnt to tune out all the noise and replace it with actually living.

The faulty body image I developed when younger which was full of cultural, societal, family and media influences, was honed over time, so it's not something we can fix overnight. However, I have begun to learn the value of nurturing and valuing my 'self' and my body, with all its 'imperfections' and despite not being my so-called 'ideal' weight. I am now able to say that I am happy in my skin for the first time in my life and I have effortlessly released over 40lbs in weight that my body no longer needs, without any dieting or food restriction of any sort.

I eat mindfully and intuitively, for example, I've learned how to tune into my body and the messages it sends me about the food it needs, how much rest or sleep it needs, how much time I need alone to re-energise myself versus how much time with other people which also energises me. I have managed to take the emotion out of food and I finally feel calm around food for the first time in my life.

I have finally learned to ask for help when I need it – this wasn't easy initially as it meant admitting I couldn't cope, and that equalled 'weakness' in my mind.

I have the most amazing, loving and supportive friends a woman could ever have, friends who just appear without being asked from all over the country. Friends who just know intuitively what I need in the way of emotional support and physical help; friends who helped me pack each time I moved and brought boxes and bubble wrap with them. Friends who cooked for me and made me eat; friends who took me to the supermarket and paid for some food shopping; friends who helped me paint my flat; friends who are always at the end of the phone and who message me every day to reassure me that someone out there cares about me; friends who have given me, and continue to give me, so much love.

I feel tremendous gratitude towards all those women who formed a safety net around me when my world fell apart, who held the space for me to heal, who gave me their spare room to sleep in when I had nowhere else to go, and who continue to be there for me to this day.

I learned that I was not alone after all and that it's ok to show vulnerability, because those who love you will still love you. Shame and fear keep us isolated but I found that sharing my fears brought arms to hold me and love to keep me strong.

Despite what we may have grown up experiencing and thinking about ourselves, we all have the power and strength to change our thoughts and behaviour with knowledge and support. We create our own reality, and if we don't like it we can choose to change it. We can choose our mood, we can choose how we react to people and situations, and we can choose to eat the food our body actually wants and the amount it needs. We can choose how we deal with stress, we can choose how we view our body when we look in the mirror, and we can choose to be happy.

I have not reinvented myself; I have become the woman I was always meant to be. And I accept myself just as I am, in all my power.

Biography

Carol May is a Transformational Health and Lifestyle Coach who uses a new understanding around the nature of the human experience, together with The Four Pillars of Lifestyle Medicine, to help midlife women suffering peri and post-menopausal issues around weight, stress, brain fog, hot flushes, overwhelm, anxiety and sleep to feel happier, calmer, more peaceful and full of energy and vitality.

In her spare time Carol enjoys performing with Rock Choir and a Classical Choir, swimming, Fitsteps, watching live music and going to the theatre.

www.allshapesandsizes.solutions

Helen Courtney

Years of systematic psychological and emotional abuse from her husband, with his multiple affairs, almost destroyed Helen's self-worth. Her public brave face was convincing, but the internal wounds and invisible scars manifested into ill health until one day her young son gave her the reason – and the strength – to leave. With support from family and friends, Helen rebuilt her confidence and her life, eventually becoming an award-winning author and healer.

From Silent Sufferer to Soulful Survivor: A Note From Me To You

Everyone has a story to tell and I am no different. I decided to share my story to raise awareness of psychological abuse, the long-term negative effects it has on a victim's sense of self, and dissolve the many incorrect myths about abuse. Statistics continually demonstrate that domestic violence is commonplace in society, so the chances are that you have personally experienced abuse or know someone who has been a victim.

Psychological abuse is a form of domestic violence. It does not discriminate age, gender, religion, job, status, or background. This form of abuse happens mainly behind closed doors, is hard to measure, can be difficult to prove and unlike physical abuse, it leaves no visible scars. There is little or no education about what non-violent abuse consists of, which is why I am so passionate about sharing my personal journey, which spanned over fifteen years. I trust that by raising awareness and through united action, together we CAN and WILL make psychological abuse a thing of the past.

I was a happy, enthusiastic, sociable, and loving child. Like most children, I looked at the world through inquisitive eyes and was innocent to certain aspects of the world around me, choosing only to see the good in people, things, and circumstances. I lived with my mother, father, older sister and budgerigar in a three-bedroom semi-detached house, until I was eight years old when we upgraded to a four-bedroom detached-house in the same small town.

My parents adopted traditional gender roles in their marriage; my mother was a 'stay at home' mum, who put her life and soul into raising me and my sister, whilst also maintaining the house and garden. My father was the provider who worked full-time to financially put a roof over our heads and support us all. I recall him being physically and emotionally absent from home for most of my childhood. For many years I instinctively knew that my mum and dad didn't have a happy marriage and appeared to live separate lives under the same roof.

When I was eleven years old, my greatest fear was realised. My mother and father announced that they were separating and getting a divorce. My mother reached her tipping point, when she discovered that my father had taken another woman on a so called 'men's holiday' to Amsterdam. I guess it was one affair too many for my mother to cope with and she somehow mustered enough strength and courage to leave.

As punishment for leaving him, my father sold our family home and no longer financially supported us. My sister decided to follow the money and moved in with my father, while my mother and I moved into a small two-bedroomed flat provided by the local council. Our new home was not ideal as it was two bus rides away from my school. It felt as though my father was fixated on degrading and inconveniencing my mother as much as possible, with little regard for how his actions impacted on my sister and me. The flat was horrid and we could smell the dampness the minute we walked through the door. The wallpaper was discoloured and peeling off the walls in numerous places. We didn't have the luxury of carpet, but instead walked on cold, hard floor tiles. With no money for furnishings, my mother pinned a bed sheet up at the window each evening as a curtain and put blankets over us to keep us warm in winter whilst watching television. My father stripped our family home of the furniture and items he wanted, so my mother had no choice but to use a garden sun lounger for my bed. I recollect the highlight of my week was being able to have a Mars bar, which we would cut into thin slices and ration.

Overnight, my life transformed from one of comfort to that of poverty. My father didn't pay child maintenance to my mother, even though he owned his own company and could afford to do so. My mother did her best to provide by working full-time, however her income was limited and after paying rent and bills, she was left with just £8.00 per week to feed us all. Despite the financial hardship, I always felt incredibly loved, cared for and supported by my mother. In contrast, I felt abandoned by, unimportant to, and unloved by my father. He didn't appear to be bothered whether he saw me or not, as his visits were inconsistent. When he did see me, it was on a Saturday and I would have to help him at work. Once we had finished for the day, it always felt as though he was clock watching for the time he could drop me back to my mother and go out for the evening. From memory, we never had quality time together and I only ever stayed overnight on one occasion and went on holiday with him once. As an eleven-year-old child, I felt deeply hurt by him and could not understand what I had done wrong.

Looking back now, I recognise that my father used me as a pawn in a game he wanted to play with my mother. Through my father's lack of attention, love, time and stability, I believe that my ability to develop a healthy relationship with men was hindered. I now understand that it is through the relationship a girl experiences with their father that a strong inner core resource, sense of well-being, healthy self-esteem and authenticity is developed. The early patterns of interaction between a father and his daughter are what the women will seek in her partner, as historic behavioural patterns become familiar. My unhealthy relationship with my father led me to seek attention in the wrong friendships and relationships.

As a teenager, I didn't have a clear sense of self and suffered from low self-esteem, lack of self-belief and deflated self-worth. I did my best to hide the inner negative beliefs about myself, however these innate feelings outwardly manifested as attempts to please others and gain their approval. I believed that I had to be a certain type of person and behave in a particular way in order to be liked, fit in, and be accepted by others. My peers had stable families, nice clothes, and the latest gadgets. I felt ashamed as my mother and father were divorced, my wardrobe limited and expensive gadgets were not a luxury my mother could afford.

When I was sixteen, I enrolled at a sixth form college to study A-levels. I saw this as a fresh start and my way of ensuring I could later secure a good job and therefore afford nice clothes, belongings and eventually a car and home. However, it was here that I became even more conscious of the aspects of my life I hated. I felt extremely self-conscious, continued to lack in confidence and believed that I had nothing to offer. A part of me was incredibly jealous of some of my peers, who were stunningly beautiful, stylish, fun and had lots to offer. My lack of self-worth and poor self-esteem resulted in me settling for any type of male attention, even when it was from unsuitable young men. Upon reflection, I realise now that my negative self-image and beliefs made me the ideal prey to a predator.

After college, I attended a local university and worked part-time at a health club to financially support myself. It was whilst working here that I met Robert, a twenty-six-year-old civil servant. Robert had a well-toned muscular physique, piercing blue eyes, a cute smile and was self-assured. At the time I believed that he was out of my league and would never be interested in someone like me. Why would he be; I was ugly and uninteresting.

Robert was extremely popular with both men and women. To men he was 'one of the lads' and to women he was a charismatic flirt. To begin with Robert and I were just friends who would socialise with other members of the gym and nothing more. During our numerous conversations, I foolishly disclosed a lot about myself, my family and past relationships. Robert was amazed to discover how I had been treated by my ex-boyfriends and couldn't understand why my first boyfriend had cheated on me. Robert was a great listener and really easy to talk to.

One evening, Robert shocked me by asking me out on a date. I knew from the rumours that Robert was a player, so I didn't want to become another one of his conquests and heartbroken casualties. I was flattered, but also cautious. My heart was telling me to go for it and yet my head was telling me to stay well clear. My heart won the internal battle and I agreed to go out with him. We had a great evening and one date turned into many. Our relationship progressed quickly and after just a few weeks, Robert introduced me to his parents. He admitted to once being a player, but assured me that those days were behind him. At twenty-six years of age, he was now ready to settle down and one day start a family. Of course, I believed him, as his words and actions at this point didn't give me any reason to doubt him.

In the beginning, our relationship was incredible. We enjoyed a good mix of nights in and nights out, as well as nights together and nights with friends. I comfortably fitted into Robert's social circle, as one of his friends had previously dated my sister and some of his other friends were members of the gym. Robert demonstrated his kind nature on multiple occasions by paying for our nights out, as he knew that my wages were limited. He was domesticated and would regularly cook meals for us at his house. He was romantic and would surprise me with small gifts, leave cute notes around the house, write hearts in ketchup on my cheese on toast and create CDs of his favourite songs for me.

After just a few months however, alarm bells started to ring in my head. His attitude and behaviour gradually began to change and my intuition was screaming at me to end the relationship. My suspicions originally started when I would uncover Robert's lies. I recall one day going to the toilet at his house and seeing a used sanitary towel in the bin. I asked Robert if he had seen anyone, but he replied that he had been on his own all day. When I pointed out that there was a used sanitary towel in his bathroom bin, Robert replied that it was his mum's. Now I know I can sometimes be a little naive, but as his mother was in her sixties I knew that she no longer menstruated. He was blatantly lying and yet I felt powerless to confront him about it, as I hated conflict. I didn't want to appear jealous or possessive, so I chose to remain silent.

In the years that followed lies would effortlessly roll off Robert's tongue, in order to purposefully cover up his infidelities. He would lie about staying over at work, but when I telephoned the station they advised me that his shift finished on time. I found long dark hairs on the pillow of our bed. I was blonde at the time! I found a lady's telephone number in his jeans pocket when washing his clothes; according to Robert he obtained it on behalf of his friend. I discovered meal receipts, calls to other women whilst I was in the bath or in bed and visits to ex-girlfriends. The list is extensive. My self-doubt, combined with Robert's accusations of paranoia, quashed my gut instincts and I became desensitised to what was happening in my relationship.

The day after my twenty first birthday, I discovered I was pregnant. Robert was over the moon and couldn't wait to announce to everyone that he was going to be a father. Although unplanned, I hoped that a baby would be the turning point in our relationship, so that we could forget the past and move forward. I was committed to doing my best for our baby and was determined to be a great mother. During the pregnancy, my life and body changed more than I thought possible. Life for Robert on the other hand didn't change at all, as he continued to go to the gym every night after work, have his weekly nights out with friends and generally did what he wanted, when he wanted.

In the spring of 1997, our daughter Freya was born and as soon as I saw her, I instantly understood what unconditional love felt like. As I cradled her carefully in my arms and looked deep into her beautiful blue eyes, I sensed my heart expand in my chest with the enormity of love I felt for her. Freya was my wonderful tiny miracle and a huge life blessing. I whispered to her that I would always love, protect, and support her, as well as accept her for who she was. I promised that I would cherish my role as her mother and that I felt honoured to be part of her life.

It didn't take long after Freya's arrival for Robert to revert to type.

Just three months after her birth, he announced that he was going on holiday with a group of friends. I discovered whilst he was away that he had told yet another lie and had gone away with one of his single mates. It was then that I realised Robert was a compulsive liar, who whole-heartedly believed his own words, and who would say and do anything to cover his tracks.

Robert's public persona was very different to the Robert I experienced behind closed doors. He had a good career and presented himself as a committed husband and dedicated father. From the outside looking in we appeared to have a lovely life and Robert was the ideal husband and father. I therefore thought it must be me and I questioned myself all the time. Maybe I expected too much from our relationship or from life in general. Maybe life was like this for everyone, but others hid it well in their pursuit of the 'perfect' life. When Freya was four years old and we were going through a good patch in our relationship, we decided to have another child. In 2002, after a traumatic pregnancy, our beautiful baby boy Drew was born.

Robert had been a very hands-on father with Freya and I automatically expected that he would be the same with Drew. I was shocked when Robert would only physically interact with Drew in the presence of others and refused to help at home. The midwife put my mind at rest however and said that many fathers struggle to adjust to another male coming into their home, so I gave Robert the space and time he needed to adapt. I remained focused on being a good mother to my children and making the most of life.

When Drew was just seven weeks old, Robert came home from work and declared that we were getting married in five weeks' time. We hadn't discussed getting married, so Robert's announcement was an utter surprise and completely out of the blue. I felt reassured that our relationship, after its numerous ups and downs, was now in a stable place. Robert was finally ready to commit to me and our family.

Just after Drew's first birthday, Robert began to return to his invalidating ways, became absent from family life and was secretive again. Every day I would tread on eggshells around him, would be anxious as I never truly knew where he was and what he was doing and I would be fearful of what lies I would unearth. I was subservient to his needs, always doing my best to please him, work hard, keep a lovely home, and raise our children.

One day, my mother collected our daughter from school and overheard two mums talking about Robert at the school gate. They didn't know who my mum was, so continued to openly discuss how fabulous they thought he was. My mum turned to them, laughed and said, "You should follow him home". My mum was usually a quiet lady, so this was completely out of character for her. However, she was angry to think that these women only saw part of who Robert truly was. They didn't see, know, or understand what life was like for me and what I endured to keep our family unit together.

I lived with and experienced the man behind the mask. At home Robert behaved as if he were king of the castle and didn't treat me as an equal. We both worked full-time and yet he expected me to do all the cooking, shopping, cleaning, washing, and ironing.

The domesticated Robert he presented himself as in the early days had vanished. Once we had moved in together, he had a clear vision of what our roles should be and defined these tasks without consultation. Robert made certain that outside of his working hours, he was free to come and go as he pleased.

My Prince Charming had turned into Prince Harming and I had turned from a Princess to Cinderella. I felt housebound, restricted, and isolated. Being a working mother, constrained to what I was able to do, where I could go and when. I became isolated from friends as Robert would often make me feel guilty for wanting to go out with them, so instead I would stay at home for an easy life.

Robert could be intimidating and in a disagreement, he would often puff out his muscular bodybuilders chest to be confrontational and ensure I backed down. Although Robert had never physically hit me, he had on a few occasions thrown things at me, like his car keys. I was always aware that a line existed between violence and non-violence and was unsure where that line was. The steroids also made his behaviour unpredictable at times. A look or a stare was all that was needed to scare me, as I knew a man of his stature could do great harm with just one punch.

He regularly invalidated me through his words and would also undermine me to the children, strategically establishing himself as good cop and me as bad cop. On the rare occasions that we went out together, he would instruct me not to embarrass him. To my knowledge I had never embarrassed him publicly or otherwise, so I became paranoid about what his friends were saying to him and what they truly thought about me. Mind games were common in our relationship too and Robert would insinuate that I was crazy and his affairs were all in my head. He would regularly go out without telling me and then when he returned home would claim that he had told me, and that either I hadn't listened or I didn't remember. Over time, I began to believe that I was going mad and would regularly question and doubt myself.

Whenever I attempted to discuss how I felt, Robert would minimise my emotions. He would often say "Oh God here we go again" or "What's wrong now? You're never happy." I became convinced that I was the problem in our marriage. I believed that I wasn't good enough, as a wife or mother. I would look in the mirror and wish I was prettier, had a better figure and could afford nicer clothes. I perceived myself as dull, boring, and predictable. I considered Robert was too good for me, as he was attractive, charming, and funny and I wondered why I ever believed our relationship would work.

In order to cope day to day, I created a mask of self-protection and preservation, which allowed me to function, perform well at work and be accepted. I wanted the world to see a happy marriage, a loving and faithful husband and devoted father. The invisible mask I wore in public cloaked my inner beliefs about myself by camouflaging my low self-esteem, lack of self- belief and waning self-worth. It disguised how lonely I was in my marriage and how scared and trapped I felt. On the outside I held my life together, whilst on the inside I was an emotional wreck. As time passed, the side-effects of Roberts abuse manifested physically as panic attacks and adrenal fatigue, my mental health suffered as I constantly functioned at high-stress levels and emotionally I felt weak and pathetic.

In cases of physical abuse, the perpetrator leaves outer physical scars which are visible evidence that the abuse occurred. However, with psychological abuse, the wounds are internal and resulting scars invisible. This somehow makes the abuse seem less real to the victim and other people. I can assure you that psychological abuse is very real indeed and imprisons the victim in a world of hopelessness. I believed that I was trapped and powerless to change my circumstances. I questioned if anyone would believe me, as Robert and I had both worn such convincing public masks.

Then, in February 2010 I awoke from my zombie-like existence and realised I had to find the strength and courage, just as my mother had done many years before me. That morning my son Drew became the reason for me to leave my dysfunctional marriage, rather than my excuse to stay.

"Stop shouting at each other, please stop shouting, you are killing me." he cried, curled up on the kitchen sofa with his hands tightly cupped over his ears, to block out the noise of Robert and me arguing. Those words echoed in my ears and were the catalyst to change my life and the life of my children.

A few months later, the children and I moved out of our family home and into rented accommodation. I had always put such a high value on owning my own home, but in the absence of love and in the presence of abuse, I had realised that a house is simply bricks and mortar. I placed a higher value on the long-term well-being of myself and my children far more than a house. I knew that if I continued in my marriage my daughter had a high chance of settling in an abusive relationship when she was older and my son could potentially repeat the patterns of his father and become an abuser. I wasn't willing for that to happen to either of my children as I loved them too much and they deserved to experience loving, caring, and balanced relationships.

Our new home represented a fresh start for us all. To me personally it symbolised freedom, hope and love. I thought leaving would be the difficult part, but in truth it was far easier than I imagined and less challenging than what was to follow. At a time when I needed the support of friends, some of the women at school chose to ignore me. I was grieving for a marriage I never experienced, hurt for my children and unsure how I would cope emotionally and financially. Some women created stories and believed gossip in preference to asking me personally why I left. It was in this time of darkness that I realised who my true friends were and recognised those whom I had to let go.

My road to recovery was rocky and I experienced many twists and turns along the way. I had good days and bad, in equal measure. I did my best to take each day one step at a time and not look too far ahead. I knew that I had been in denial for so many years and had much learning, grieving, and healing to do. My support network was pivotal in my recovery. My mother, family and friends were amazing, by offering a listening ear and their invaluable time. By going out, visiting friends for tea or simply chatting on the phone, I felt like a normal human being.

It was clear just how upset for me my family and friends were and how they wanted to help me. However, I had to take responsibility for my own healing, as this wasn't something that they could do for me. I engaged with professionals who could help me to transform my limiting beliefs about myself, heal the emotional and mental wounds that had been created by the abuse and provide me with empowerment tools that would enable me to be emotionally resilient and have a positive self-image. The therapy environment allowed me to feel safe, so that I could explore my inner world and heal physically, emotionally, and mentally. Therapy wasn't a quick fix, but it was a long-term solution that I was willing to persevere with. I regularly attended therapy sessions and after each one, I could feel the positive changes that were taking place within me. Each and every day, I was becoming stronger and developing a sense of self.

By healing my inner wounds, I was able to move on, rebuild my life and trust again. I met and married my soul mate and life partner, who had also experienced abuse. We both had a natural understanding, appreciation and empathy for what the other had experienced. Scott and I agreed that we did not want the shadows of the past to negatively influence our relationship, so we engaged with a Couples Counsellor to give our relationship a solid foundation on which we could build. My marriage to Scott has taught me so much and fully restored my faith in men, as he is loving, trustworthy, funny, romantic, kind and encouraging. Our relationship is balanced and together, we work through any challenges that life throws at us.

Today, I am able to look back at my first marriage with understanding rather than bitterness and hate. I am grateful first and foremost for the wonderful children that I am blessed with, as a result of my relationship with Robert. I am also appreciative of the learning experiences Robert gave me, as the abuse encouraged me to seek professional support.

As a result, I healed my internal wounds and blossomed into the person I always wanted to be. I no longer strive for perfection or compare myself to others. I am happy to be me and value my inner and outer beauty, skills and fundamentally the core person I am.

As a direct result of my life experiences and challenges, I retrained and set up my own business. Today, I am privileged to support women to break free of their negative self-beliefs, recover from challenges, be emotionally resilient and live to their potential. Our divorce also gave me the opportunity to make the transition through the separation without using our children as a pawn and as a result, I am now able to help parents avoid relationship battles and put their children's needs before their own to secure their long-term wellbeing.

My life today illustrates that we are not defined by our past experiences, we have the ability to transform our lives by transforming our inner selves, as happiness is an inside job.

Today I am no longer a silent sufferer. I am a 'Soulful Survivor!'

Biography

Helen has helped women in her private practice and through workshops over the past six years; locally, nationally and internationally. Using traditional coaching techniques alongside metaphysical practices, Helen enables women to clear emotional blockages, subconscious limiting beliefs and restrictive patterns of behaviour at root source. Helen facilitates graceful connection to a woman's inner resources and power, aiding her clients to fully align to their inner source of confidence, belief, worth and self-love. From a place of self- security and emotional resilience, women are able to develop soulful nurturing habits, connect to their intuition and live authentic, purposeful and limitless lives. In 2015, Helen won the 'Best Healer' Award with Health and Happiness Magazine for her therapy work, as well 'Best Author' Award with Women Inspiring Women for her debut book *The Silent Sufferer*. In 2016, Helen went onto win the 'Most Inspiring Person' Award with Health and Happiness magazine for her charity work 'Helping Handbags', which helped over 3,000 homeless women in the West Midlands, Birmingham and Worcester areas.

The Silent Sufferer is available from www.amazon.co.uk
www.helencourtney.co.uk

Sam Geddes

Like so many young, naïve women, Sam wanted to be loved, to feel whole – yet lust brought her to a place of passion, terror, self-hatred and 'un-living'. Planning her escape took a year. Depression set in, inspite of her children and loving new husband. Writing about her life one day was powerful; she felt completely renewed, and now her mission is to show others how they can see the magic in everyday life.

The Unlikely Warrior

Our house rested upon an ancient Welsh hill, neither up nor down. It was rumoured Boudicca walked these lands and that her body now lay silent within the Gop, a burial mound just a short walk from here. It was whispered amongst the villagers that when the wind howled you could hear the screams and cries of battles fought, I knew better, they were my sounds not soldiers of the past, spilling out of this place which constantly fought to be a home but was always a prison.

I had been petrified all day.

What if anyone called and realised what I was doing? Please, nobody, stop me. I begged to the sky.

As I looked back at the house, it was tired. Tired of dreaming of being something it would never be, of the laughter broken by the banging, breaking, and crying noises that shook its foundations almost daily. The pebbledash seemed blacker, cracks wider and the front door which had tried so many times to let me out, bent and split open, where he had forced it shut.

I felt sad and happy. Sad that I could not fulfil the dreams of making this house a home, it had such potential; we had such potential, and happy that I was escaping, leaving to make a new home, just me and the kids; free.

Lust had brought me here, all those years ago. Those deep dark brown eyes I almost fell into, an older guy, so very different, I thought, from the boys I had hung round with most of my teenage life.

I was mesmerised by the depth and twinkle of those eyes as he glanced across at me, along with his sultry smile, it had caught me off guard and had drawn me in, tempting me with what I thought was a more grown up love. We played about at first, neither one of us knowing or realising the consequences we were about to plough into for the rest of our young adulthood. The lust was like a spell, but no fairy godmother cast this, the devil was at work here.

My mind still scatters seeking out good memories of us; I have not yet reached that part of my mind, but I find that any flashbacks now make me smile rather than shudder with fear, mostly of time with the children, we looked like such a happy family.

His mother once asked me why I continued to bother with him as

I drove from their home in tears. Love hurts I guess.

Dancing, there was dancing. I always wanted someone who could dance, and together we moved gracefully as we gazed lovingly into each other's eyes, and in those moments all that had gone before didn't matter, it was like a reset button.

Perhaps the afternoon we made love in the woods amongst the blue bells…but that is just a hazy memory dressed up with glitter, it really wasn't that great.

I could continue to plug the gaps between that hate with love, but there is very little love within a relationship that feeds a vampire, whether they are born as one or are bitten to behave as one. Any love is drained like blood from the victim's neck to feed an insatiable, unquenchable thirst. I look back and scrutinise my actions as a young woman, like WHAT was I thinking?! I know now of course that so much of me was missing already, even before I fell into this deep dark hole. I was looking for fulfilment, to be loved. I expected to fall into the happy-ever-after and what I got was most definitely the Grimm version of the fairy tale, warts and all.

All of my mistakes slapped me in my face all at once: Saying yes when I meant "No." Betraying my soul mate, kissing someone else's boyfriend, staying silent when I could have spoken up, allowing people to bully me, and bullying others. Stealing from the bright lights of the happy, tuneful machine in Kwik Save's foyer (my hand was teeny-tiny enough to slip all the way through the trough to take my pick of colourful surprise filled eggs).

Telling the deputy head at school to go shove his child development class up his ass, because all I ever wanted to do was mechanics, which I should have done. Not singing.

Doing as I was told, then rebelling in completely the wrong way, like not even 'fun' rebelling, but seriously stupid mistakes, rebelling that really was no fun at all.

Thinking another person made me whole.

The list was endless. Was I a bad person? It felt like it. I was being punished. It was all that I needed to help add fuel to his venomous torrent of verbal fire.

I hated myself. I felt like I was nothing.

Everything I did led me here, to say goodbye to what could have been home forever, but the reality was, if I stayed I would be laying silent there along with Boudicca; we had both fought our last battle, yet the outcome would have been so very different for me.

It hadn't been the first time I had wanted to go. The thoughts raced through my head often faster and louder than the screams I unleashed when I wished it would all stop. I couldn't go, there was too much history embedded in me, in the frustrations of my ancestors, the children; "you must stay for the children", that is what you are supposed to do. Rules, restrictions, society and the voices of old crones, with traditional values crashing around in my head. They were holding the key to my prison and waving it in my face like some jewel I must win and not just be given.

I was so broken by it all. The fear of going outweighed that of staying. I knew everything about being there, but walking out of that door, well it was another battlefield for which I didn't feel I had the strength. It wasn't just the voices in my head that beat me, it was his voice too. If he wasn't hurling bitter words, spitting profanities, and screaming in my ear what a 'bitch' I was, how 'shit' I was (oh how my ears still ring with pain from those words), he was pleading for forgiveness and promising me 'never again'. It was a constant battle of wills, within him and with me, that created perpetual confusion, an inconclusive state, with no one winning and everyone losing. Each and every day, with all my might I focused hard to take in the words, ensuring I had heard them correctly, so as to spit them back at him in the hope he would realise his errors and love me like he was supposed to. It took me way too long to know deep down this was never happening and I was not loved.

It had become more and more obvious to me that this state of 'un-living' was going to kill me, more perhaps than an unfortunate accident brought about by the consequences of an uncontrollable anger. I had pains in my chest daily, I cried most mornings with the frustrations of simple everyday life, I shouted at the kids, oh god no, I screamed at them. This was not me.

I cast my mind back to a previous escape (there had been several more) when I had up and gone for days. I was peering out of a bedroom window in my Mother's old house, as he returned the car that he had "ripped the heart out of" two nights before, because I had decided it wasn't a good idea to stay with him when he was so drunk. Fortunately, in that battle I had driven over his leg accidentally, giving me enough of a gap to call for help. I went back of course. That time.

This time I had planned my escape. Neatly in a little book, with everything I needed to do to leave and all I wanted to do to create a new life for myself. It had once been remarked that I would know when the day had come to leave, the day when I would no longer accept that this was my fate. That day had arrived; I had woken up one morning and said to myself "no more of this", and with that decision made, it would be followed. It is only when I look back on this momentous decision that I feel incredibly strong and courageous. It took almost a year to implement the plan. My nerves jumped more than usual expecting him to notice things slowly disappearing, that he may find my neat little book, rip it to pieces and laugh or answer my phone to an estate agent instead of me. Despite all this stuff happening he was totally unaware that I seemed a lot happier than usual. It was a little like being hidden behind a cloaking device.

The kids never questioned me, ever. I spoke to them, they knew each step we were taking, they knew where we were going; it was a risk, but I wanted to tell them and they never uttered a word to him, like they knew the inevitable. It gave me complete reassurance it was time to go.

I was creating a new home and it was fun. I could feel the chains around my wrists ease as I made more and more decisions of my own. I hadn't had a proper kitchen in two years, maybe longer. It was part of the many 'adjustments' he had made to the house. There was a tap sticking out of the lounge wall, with a bucket and a 'Baby Belling' cooker, which at first was a little like camping; novel, but as time went on getting home from work at six every evening and cooking for the family, together with making a coal fire for hot water, is nay near impossible. It was one of the reasons why I had chosen a newly built house, in a cul-de-sac, with three bedrooms, a family bathroom; I even had an en-suite. Best of all a separate lounge, cosy yet perfect, and an all singing all dancing kitchen diner, bliss! I had never wanted a kitchen so much in all my life. There was a conservatory and a garden too; compared to 'home' it was paradise for us all. We came straight from school, everything ready for them to feel right at home; a new family, a real home. I felt euphoric.

Yet every part of me trembled for weeks after, while I waited, like a new recruit on their first frontline encounter. I was filled with disbelief.

How long before he realises we are gone? How long before he finds me again?

Time moved like treacle.

The phone rang and rang for hours. It was him. I will not pick it up. I'm not ready for the next battle; I want a moment more to wallow in my new paradise…please?

Like any who have survived a prolonged tour of combat, the experience lingered like rotten eggs that had been left to fester in the trenches, where battle cries still echoed. Living, and reliving them for the first time, my mind was a mess. I wished for Boudicca; if like her, I could yield a sword, my battle would be won in one fell swoop, whether me or him, it would end. Now though, our sword yielding days are long gone, and it is the battle within me that needed to be endured and conquered.

It was time to leave, again. My plan had failed. Well of sorts, I had remained true but I had overlooked the need to drive more land between the past and this new life. I needed far more oxygen.

We drove for hours late into the night. The car was packed to the hilt, hardly room for the kids, yet we had left so much behind. Every time a police car went by my stomach fluttered fiercely in case they noticed and pulled us over. I was panicking, random thoughts had raced through my mind. What if it triggered a call to HQ? Then they would find out we had done another runner. He could have said anything. We had left Maggie the cat behind too and I felt guilty; my daughter was her best friend in the whole world. He had found the cuddly cat, on Halloween no less; it was bigger than my daughter's head, black and white and so very soft. It hadn't been out of her arms since, the love was unconditional, and she celebrated Maggie's birthday each Halloween in a completely witchy style. A tear slid down my face as I pondered on why a father could be so loving and yet to me so cruel. I wasn't yet sure how we would retrieve her, but we would.

Leaving the first time had been easier, I was sure. This time I had taken far more from the children. They were slightly older, more aware, bonds with friends so much stronger. My daughter was furious, I knew it. Just starting high school was not the time to rip her away, and she would ensure I felt her pain. The youngest was yet to understand; at four he was quite happily on an adventure.

All these thoughts haunted me, as I blinked my way along the never-ending motorway, I couldn't fathom all I had to leave behind to be safe, like a soldier, once more forced to make choices between who and what to leave behind in order to survive.

I was now two hundred and twenty-three miles from home. I had left the country I had known all my life, as it seemed apparent that he would never comprehend that "No" meant "NO" or accept that I was no longer with him. I wrenched myself from certainty to uncertainty; ironically the latter felt slightly safer. I am in England, it's foreign territory, different people, no one knows me. I don't know me. It is all overwhelming. The move, everyone squished into a bachelor's pad, little confused faces, new schools, and a dark cloud hanging over me that not even a hurricane could blow away.

I had put on a brave face, too long the pains within me brewing unresolved, my body knowing much more than I was aware of; it had taken it upon itself to decide this was a safe spot to just collapse. And so, I did. I lay in bed, the duvet firmly fixed around my body, I couldn't get up. I couldn't hold down a job. I couldn't be a mother. The sadness washed over me. Euphoria was gone. Smog was filling my brain, suffocating my senses. I couldn't feel, I was numb.

I was still shackled. The door had opened to my freedom but I hadn't quite got all the way out. How long would this last? This was not what I was expecting at all.

The plan was: Get away.

Live a new life.

It will all be fine.

The shock had finally hit. I hadn't experienced anything close to this before. It wasn't just twelve years of abuse bringing me to the floor, it was almost thirty years of being lost, suppressed, controlled and conforming to all the things I was supposed to be, to do, and yet felt unable to do. I was to realise that it was not that I wasn't capable, but my true spirit was knocking furiously from within shouting, screaming, asking, although I couldn't hear with all the outside noise: "Please, let me out". This was going to take considerable time.

Much to my bafflement, I was not to be alone in this process. My love would prod me gently; make suggestions, let's go out, what about a shower? The fates had brought him to me.

It would take a while, and a few more traumas, before I would stand on my own two feet again. I read books, I fell in love, I read books, I worked, I got married, I read books, I got bullied at work, I read books, I had a baby, I got ill, I read books, I got better, I started my own business, I read a serious amount of books.

Depression lingered.

Life was supposed to be bliss. Smog. Numb. Confused.

Days would go by and I had done nothing but stare into space. My sleeve often soggy by the daily torrent of tears that I felt came from nowhere but brought much. I knew I had to be here, but it lacked familiarity, and friends who had been an immense support once, were now silent, the distance making it easy to forget how much we had all been a part of each other's lives. Even with the children, who loved regardless and a now husband who wanted to make it all better, I felt incredibly alone.

Depression is like that. Isolating.

Secretly creeping up on you, and before you recognise it, you are consumed by the poison of sadness, despite being the ever optimistic person you thought you were. We were to play a game, depression and I; there would be battle of wills and wits, and then if I learned something I would be allowed a reprieve, maybe three or six months and then it would pull me back in to the depths of despair, even though I thought there could be no more to learn. Oh, but there was!

It was difficult to forget those twelve years. The flashbacks were often more fierce than the reality. There were no excuses for that kind of behaviour. I believed some people were evil and some were not; whether by choice or not, some behaved only as they were able to, and so I learned to forgive. It was a humbling feeling. I would look at myself in the mirror. Dark circles had formed under my eyes as if to remind me of the darkness I still had to battle with. Wrinkles tell stories, eyes tell the truth, I thought.

My heart was empty.

I felt like I had lost my anchor on a treacherous voyage, but I knew I would need to sail all the way back through my life to find it. How was I to find my way? A lighthouse, I needed a lighthouse. Amongst the smog and salty air, I raised my telescope in a bid to seek out this lighthouse. I was almost blinded with her 'angel-like' glow, her gaze soft, yet I knew there was no fooling her, she had known me far too long. It was her undeniable strength and wisdom that was to flow into my very essence like an antidote to the sad poison I had drunk, that would steer me toward the nuggets of treasure I required to fill my heart up with joy.

Depression tightened its grip. Not this time, I yelled. Buckle up foe, we are about to become friends. I wrote furiously from the waters of my mind, it was illegible, but I didn't need to re-read these words, I was lightening the load so I could sail full steam ahead. I battled demons I had no consciousness of; I tussled with blame, guilt and incredible shame, all their guts spilt out for the craziest of autopsies. As I wrote through seas of tears, the smog began to clear and I caught sight of a forgotten place. I found myself barefoot, the ground caressing my feet; where had I fallen, upon what and whom?

There, sat on an old oak tree stump was a young girl, dressed in an intricately made lilac fairy dress; her face was fair, freckles delicately scattered across her pixie nose, feet bare and muddy, hair auburn and wild. She glowed like a sunbeam and you could tell she was in her element, innocently exploring the mini world around her with eyes wide open. A magical tingle flew like fairy dust over every inch of my body. My heart started thudding loudly; so much that I was worried she would hear me. She did not. Her world was far from mine, yet this vision felt like a memory.

I sat still for a moment and looked up at the sky. It was the bluest sky I had ever seen, no cloud in sight. The birds chirped happily in the trees, it was like I was hearing them for the first time. My heart began to settle into a rhythm like it had found its orchestra. I noticed how energised I felt, sat there on the earth, barefoot. I took a big breath, the sweet-smelling air filled my lungs, I felt renewed.

The smog had completely lifted.

I peered into a small pool of water and stared at my reflection. My face was fair, freckles delicately scattered across my 'not-so' pixie nose. I looked towards my bare muddy feet and back again to see my wild auburn hair. The little sunbeam was me. I had come full circle, navigated to the very heart of who I was. It all made sense. I had unknowingly chosen all of these battles, yet, I had the strength to not only fight, but come out the other side more beautiful, with wisdom that made my heart so full, it enabled me to keep the magic of it with me every day and freely allow it to spill over to share.

I had found my truth.

A real warrior does not lead with a sword.

She leads with a wise spirit, enormous embracing heart, and an extraordinary inner-strength, which is incomparable with any brute force or devilish hand. Her vibrant energy sourced from the very nature from which she was born.

You would not know it; she had not known it. And here I am, The Unlikely Warrior.

Biography

Sam is a writer, storyteller and teacher. You will find her wandering the wilderness in Wiltshire, hunting down the closest beach, often with her four children in tow, and seeking out the magic in every day. Sam writes about her journey, about life, and healing and all the messy glorious wisdom that comes from it. She is Founding Editor of *Catching Life Magazine*, where she invites 'Mindful Misfits' to voice their messy, glorious stories and explore what they want to feel, be and do in the world. This acts as a platform to share her mission to show others how they can see the everyday magic in life, even after traumatic life experiences, and contribute to creating a world that works with Mother Nature and not against her, whilst being incredibly beneficial for our mind, body and soul.

www.samanthageddes.com
www.catchinglife.co.uk
www.survivedv.org.ukRefuge.org.uk
www.nspcc.org.uk
www.freedomprogramme.co.uk
The Chimp Paradox by Dr Steve Peters
Twelve Lessons by Kate Spencer *Daring Greatly* by Brene Brown

Susie Mackie

Obedience, conformity, and humiliation at school created in Susie, a sensitive, creative girl, low self-worth and a need to continually justify her existence. Thinking that love would complete her, yet susceptible to attracting 'unsuitable' boyfriends, led her into disastrous marriages. The lessons of life have not come easy, but Susie has finally reached a place of self-belief, rejoices in her inner strength, and uses her experiences to empower others. Her mission? To help women, whatever their age or circumstance, to not only see but also know their true worth.

"YOU CAN'T LEAVE ME. YOU PROMISED TO OBEY."

Who else promised to obey their husbands in their wedding ceremony? Why did we do this? My reason was to show him that I was placing my trust in him – that he would never actually call upon this vow of obedience. How naïve can a woman be?

I had a privileged background, lovely home on a Hampshire dairy farm, private all girls' school, horses, all the trappings of a wonderful childhood.

I was taught, both at home and at school, to respect my elders simply because they were my elders. That in itself is not necessarily a bad thing, but why should my elders treat me disrespectfully, sometimes cruelly, and demand that they be respected unconditionally?

School was ruled by fear and was one of the most negative and unfulfilling periods of my life. Humiliation was doled out publicly to both staff and pupils. Frowns were ever-present on the faces of the two Principals; nail inspection results and deportment marks posted on the corridor walls; obedience and conformity were demanded. When I left at the age of sixteen I didn't have an assertive bone in my body. Not knowing what I wanted to do with my life, I embarked on a two-year secretarial course, when in reality the last thing I wanted to be was a secretary. The best bit about this was the three hours spent every Wednesday afternoon learning Cordon Bleu cookery; it fed my creative nature, and was a skill which would later prove useful.

I seemed to attract 'unsuitable' boyfriends. I had so much to give, but ultimately, my relationships were with men who were either emotionally or physically abusive – or both – and my self-worth simply spiralled lower with each 'failure'.

At twenty-seven I married an army Captain whose mother told me she was "happy he had found someone to serve him". Only too glad to have found someone who wanted me, I was perfectly willing to offer myself up to him. We lived on camp in Northern Ireland during the troubles, and he was away a lot.

He would be angry with me for renting a £1.50 video when there was 'only me' to watch it. I was criticised for having the heating on while there was 'only me' in the house, so used to sit with a duvet around me and a hot water bottle on my lap to keep me warm. I swear it rained every sodding day that year in Ireland! So there I was, obeying to the point of self-sacrifice. The man I thought was strong and caring was in fact a bully. I internalised my stress, became very ill, and was on medication for migraines and ulcers. I can remember sitting on the floor in the corner of our bedroom, just rocking. I felt worthless and unlovable. The end for me was when we were discussing having children. He was in the bath, and I had brought him a cup of tea. I happened to mention that I had chatted with my mother about my desire to have children soon – I was twenty-eight and didn't want to wait too long. He was angry that I had discussed this with my mother! At that moment something in me snapped, and I told him I wanted a divorce. His response was to throw the hot tea in my face. Quickly rinsing my face under the cold tap, I was too shaken to speak, but remember knowing, that moment, that our marriage was over.

I managed to leave with my father's help, even though my husband told me I couldn't leave because in our wedding service I had "promised to obey". At that time, all I wanted was to end a bad marriage. As he was an Army officer, I didn't want his career to be upset by a divorce due to his 'bad behaviour' and I didn't ask for anything, I just left with what had belonged to me. Would I do things differently now? Possibly. It is one thing to walk away with your dignity, which I managed to hold onto, but another to allow a bully's actions to go unanswered. That, for me, had to come much later. Standing up to the bully has been one of the most empowering and necessary elements of recent years. Once mastered, the change from within is powerful.

My second marriage, a few years later, was also to a Captain in the army, a very different kind of man and everyone loved him. Everything seemed fine for a while. We were posted to Germany and life on camp ticked on. My husband spent time away but I knew that this was par for the course and although for months at a time I was in essence a single mum, I had a great neighbour with a baby the same age and we spent a lot of time together – the children adored each other and we had our own little support system.

We left the army when our daughter was a year old, and three months later my husband was offered a job in the Middle East. I can remember arriving in Oman and being so excited, but also feeling like a fish out of water. Everything seemed so alien, and the intense heat and humidity were a real shock to the system. Things were ok, my husband's working hours were long, and as an expat wife I couldn't work, so I studied interior design by correspondence. Oman wasn't a very healthy place to be, you could see the pollution from all the oil tankers as a brown cloud sitting on the horizon, and the old air conditioning systems in our flat caused numerous viruses, one which affected my breathing, tracheitis, accurately described by my doctor as 'like breathing broken glass'. Another caused the pigment in my retina to leak resulting in loss of half the sight in one eye, and then a miscarriage. The latter was especially traumatic, being so far away from home, but expat friends very quickly become close friends, and I had wonderful support and understanding. I had just enrolled on the interior design course, yet I couldn't see properly to butter my toast let alone draw a straight line! Fortunately, three months later it corrected itself and, throwing myself into the course with my usual enthusiasm, I earned a Diploma with merit.

Our expat life was an easy life in many ways; very social, with fantastic opportunities to explore the country. Our close-knit group of friends also loved to explore, and our adventures wadi and dune bashing were amazing fun, if at times pretty hairy! It was here I developed a love of photography – Oman was a beautiful place and the three years we spent there were a major part of my life. My husband worked hard, he was very bright, and with the advent of the internet he spent a lot of time on it. It was horrifying to discover that he was engaging in a lot of internet porn and chat lines. I felt deeply betrayed and less than enough to make him happy, and so, once back in the UK, we went to Relate for counselling. I can remember the counsellor very firmly asking, "Susie, why are you still justifying yourself all the time?"

At Christmas 2000 I became ill with flu – for the third Christmas running. The emotional stresses – and keeping these under wraps – were taking their toll. We were living in our dream home, a cottage which we lovingly nurtured back to life from its derelict state, and my family was everything to me. This time, however, I ended up in hospital with pericarditis, inflammation of the lining of the heart, and developed pneumonia; my husband was told I was 'gravely ill'. Being confronted with your own mortality is frightening; I remember waking up in hospital in the early hours and being so scared of dying – the sight of my two forlorn little girls standing at the ambulance doors waving me goodbye is burnt into my brain; there was no way I was going to leave them behind. Balanced with the need to justify my existence, there was a deep determination to make life good, and I've always worked hard for this. I recovered, but pushed myself too hard, too soon; six weeks later I was back doing presentations for a direct sales fashion company. I was soon diagnosed with M.E., myalgic encephalomyelitis, a chronic, fluctuating, neurological condition that causes symptoms affecting many body systems, more commonly the nervous and immune systems. The next two years, with my husband now working in London during the week, were hugely challenging. My weight plummeted to seven and a half stone, and I had so little strength I would have to climb the stairs on my hands and knees. Friends were amazing, as were my daughters, but it was Dr Mark Atkinson in London who was the one to get me back on my feet again. He told me that those with M.E. were driven, didn't know when to stop, that our mind isn't just in our head, it's in our whole body, and that we need to listen to our mind and what our body is trying to tell us. He also said that every single person who ends up with M.E. has had childhood trauma. That figures!

My husband and I were in counselling for nearly a year. We were due to finish the week before I discovered that for the past six months he had been having an affair. I discovered this when he had gone to London one morning and I called his mobile. It answered without him realising. His lover was just getting into his car, I heard their greeting, and their long kiss. I knew then what it felt like to be punched, very hard, in the stomach. Literally doubled over with pain, I shouted his name again and again down the phone, but he couldn't hear me. The shock of discovering the affair – both in this way, and after what I had believed was a worthwhile and successful journey through a year's counselling together – was devastating.

Then followed a long and dreadful time in my life, and for my daughters. Our eldest was thirteen, and hated him and didn't want me to fight for the marriage, which I did for five weeks. I never thought I would do this if my husband was unfaithful. Would I now? Absolutely not! Our youngest was ten, and she didn't want him to go. I had two daughters with completely polarised views, and I will never forget the three of us standing in the kitchen in a huddle, arms around each other, weeping. So much trauma followed, upset after upset. On the day my daughters and

I were moving out of our home, he stopped the sale. He now lives there at weekends with his partner. Not the woman he left me for – she had ended it. And at that time he told me we should start afresh, although he would want her as a friend and that meant seeing her and hugging her and I would have to get used to that…somehow, I found the strength to move away and move on.

My neighbour introduced me to her nephew. I was still vulnerable but he made me laugh, really laugh, spontaneously and often, and that felt so good after so much pain. Two years later we married; he drank a fair bit but I thought if he had me, surely he wouldn't need to drink so much. Who identifies with that one? We lived in his mother's house which seemed a win-win situation for us all. However, sadly not for the first time, he and his mother fell out, and he sought solace from the bottle. For the last eighteen months we were there, his mother didn't speak to me. That really hurt; my home didn't feel like my home anymore, but just the place she allowed us to live. College was a sanctuary and a constant through all this; I completed my photography degree with a First, and found my passion – photographing people and helping them feel better about themselves. To be honest I think this saved my sanity.

His mother ordered us to leave her house so we rented a farmhouse. Making wherever I am into 'home' has always been my coping mechanism, and once again I put my energy – and money – into creating a home for us all, but after a only year my husband fell out with our landlord who gave us notice. My husband's anger frightened my youngest daughter, and I knew it was time to leave. We had spent the last three years of our marriage in separate bedrooms. I was so lonely that I used to hold my own hand in bed at night; there is nothing as lonely as feeling totally alone in your marriage. I also felt incredibly guilty that I had put my daughters through so much. Thankfully they have blossomed into beautiful, talented, loving young women, and we are very close. They are my greatest pride and a constant source of joy. In September 2012, once again my parents helped me leave and set up home in a cottage near Ledbury, a perfect sanctuary for my youngest and me.

So, having married three men with either addictive or controlling personalities, and endured so much pain and unhappiness, it was time to take stock. As I was once told, if you don't learn the lesson, the lesson keeps coming to you. Yup, that's certainly true. Pushing myself consistently too hard and ignoring my 'body-mind' resulted in further illness, eventual collapse, two lots of eye surgery to save the sight, and fibromyalgia. Being told by the doctor that there was no cure for the pain of the latter, that I would have to live with it and 'manage' it, made me all the more determined not to! Yet my experiences have ultimately made me strong; I own the part I played in them, understand why I allowed my fundamental niceness to be abused, and now I believe in my worth – with the help of sheer determination, my family, friends and my career. I no longer simply survive; I thrive. I bear no anger or ill will towards my ex- husbands. I meet the most wonderful people through my business and many of my clients have become friends. I'm respected, admired and loved – all a huge boost to my self-worth.

If I hadn't been through these experiences I wouldn't be doing what I am now. And what I do now – help women build their self-worth, really know their value – gives meaning to all those traumatic experiences of my past. I use my experiences, my camera and my empathy, with a good dose of humour, to give my clients an empowering and confidence building experience. This enables them to leave me walking tall, with eyes shining. With a boudoir shoot, the empowering experience of the shoot leaves my clients feeling transformed, liberated and confident. Perhaps it sounds a little far-fetched, but some even say their boudoir shoot has changed their lives. Naturally, this makes me extremely happy – as well as validated.

I now give presentations and run workshops and retreats to inspire and enable women to become self-empowered. I love helping women to become truly, deeply confident in who they are as women, regardless of their situation, background, career, age, size, shape, indeed any external circumstances – it is, after all, about the woman within, self-acceptance, and her innate sense of 'self'.

In his powerful classic 'The Road Less Travelled', M. Scott Peck wrote "…it is essential for therapists to bring to their relationship with patients a total capacity for openness and truthfulness. How can a patient be expected to endure the pain of confronting reality unless we bear the same pain? We can only lead insofar as we go before."

So, for me, while I am not a therapist, it's about empathy – I've been there, and I know only too well the consequences low self-worth has on your whole life, on the choices you make, and the unhealthy relationships you suffer. The impact of these affects not only you, but your children – those you have, and indeed, those who are yet to be born. I once read that the best thing parents can do for their children is to love each other. So, if low self-worth leads to making a poor choice of partner, the consequences can be sadly ongoing.

Confidence is not a given. It is not an entity. It's a state of mind, even a state of being. It comes from acceptance of your body and mind (self-esteem), and feelings of wellbeing and belief in your abilities, skills and experience (confidence). At fifty-nine, I am in the best place ever. I choose to live with love. I choose to be more conscious, to honour my emotions and work with the flow of life, rather than live with anything that is second best. I believe it is never too late to find your 'self', your passion, and to build a bright, secure and happy future.

> Life isn't about finding yourself. Life is about creating yourself.
> George Bernard Shaw

Biography

October 2023 Update!
Where have the past six years gone?!

In 2019 I published the second volume of 'Women of Spirit': twenty-nine more incredible stories!

Life has thrown some more curveballs, as it has for many. Sadly both my parents have died, but they were a great age and went gently into their night.

I had eight days in hospital with Covid and nearly died. Long Covid for a year, but am thankful to be (mostly) better now.

A legal battle since the day my mother died is not quite over some thirty-two months later, but from the (horrendous) experience I will be writing a book on how to avoid the emotional trauma, the legal pitfalls, and the huge financial drain that such a case can bring.

And I've been busy!

Moving forward with female empowerment, I've become a Licensed

Mental Toughness Assessor, partnering with AQR International. I've created 'Mental Toughness for the Female Mindset' and 'Mastering Mental Toughness' workshops for companies - going into the corporate world for the first time at the age of sixty-five. Exciting - it's never too late! Next year I will launch an online course for individuals.

I've been incredibly fortunate to have earned some accolades and awards:

Fellow of the Royal Society of Arts.
Corporate Social Responsibility Award Runner Up 2023 Women's Business Club.
Awarded 'Resilience Warrior 2022' by SMBN.
Ladies First Professional Development 'Advocate for Women' Award 2018.
Woman & Home Magazine Amazing Women Awards 2019, finalist in recognition of work encouraging women to 'make their world a better place', from which the sponsors, Hotter Shoes, made me one of their 'Inspirational Women'.
G100 Chair Gloucestershire Region, Health and Wellness Wing.

My girls are just amazing and following their dreams, one a wonderful healer and breathwork facilitator, (website below) and one an outdoor adventure instructor currently loving life in New Zealand. I am immensely proud of them both and the love we share is just the best.

Best place to find me and connect with me is here:

https://www.linkedin.com/in/susiemackieadvocateforwomen
www.susiemackielife.com
www.womenofspirit.co.uk
https://www.g100.in
https://www.actionforme.org.uk
https://www.naturallylottie.com

Lacey Thompson

According to the NHS, around one in five hundred mothers will suffer from postpartum psychosis. This is not just the 'baby blues', it's a serious mental illness and should be treated as a medical emergency. It's hard to even begin to imagine what Lacey and her family went through with this illness. Lacey has been incredibly open in sharing the details of her illness and the impact it's had on her and her family: so very brave, and I salute the whole family for how they have confronted almost unthinkable challenges after the birth of a baby.

The moment I saw my daughter for the very first time back in September 2015, the overwhelming rush of love was unexplainable. There were not enough words in the English dictionary that could describe how much I loved her. The first few months of being a new mum was hard of course but wonderful, and I felt as though I'd found my calling in life - and that was to be her mummy!

My burning ambition in life was to become a midwife so, when my daughter was two, I went back to college to re-do my GCSE's then went on to do my A levels at the age of twenty-six. I achieved great results and all my hard work payed off as I secured a place at university, starting my midwifery degree in September 2018. However, life had other plans, the second day of university I had the most devastating news. I was pregnant. This was definitely not the plan; I wanted my degree not a baby. After a lot of thought I decided to carry on with my course, take a year out then return once the baby was a year old.

I achieved great results both in the theory and placement and fell even more in love with midwifery. The pregnancy was straight forward, but I felt no connection towards the baby; I did not believe I was pregnant - I looked pregnant, but I did not feel it. Every time the baby moved, I thought I had trapped wind. Looking back, I knew then that my mood was low, but I didn't have time to realise it, what with exams, deadlines, and long placement hours as well as a three-year-old. University was stressful, but I loved every second of it. I brought forward all my deadlines to finish the first year by the time the baby had arrived.

But again, life had other plans. Six weeks before my due date, whilst on placement and in surgery assisting in a cesarean section, my waters broke. After two days of staying in hospital I caught sepsis and was induced into labour. I had a very long, very painful, and very intense labour. Twenty hours in my body decided it was time to push despite only being seven centimetres dilated. With my legs up high and a doctor in between them things took a turn for the worst. The red buzzer was pulled, and words flew around the room. Being a student midwife, I knew what most of the words meant, and they were not good. The decision was made to get the baby out and as quickly as possible, I was cut with no pain relief and the baby arrived seconds later.

It was a boy; he let out a small whimper which was a good sign, but his breathing declined rapidly. He was taken to intensive care, put in an incubator and given assistance with his breathing. I sat hopelessly next to the incubator for three weeks, with constant alarms, flashing lights and scary moments. When he finally came home, I felt like I was doing amazingly with two children; I took both of them out every day and was breast feeding on the go.

Then the crying started. The baby cried twenty-four hours a day, he wouldn't settle and would not be comforted. He would cat nap for ten minutes a time, then wake up screaming again. I took him to the doctors again and again, telling them there was something wrong with this baby. My daughter would say: "He is broken, can we put him back?". This carried on for four weeks, I was sleep deprived and frustrated. Finally, he was diagnosed with a severe milk allergy, yet by this point my mood was extremely low. But, yet again, I didn't have time to realise this. Once the milk was changed to completely dairy free, he became better quite quickly and he soon was a happy healthy baby.

As the baby got better and better my mood became lower and lower. I began to leave him on the floor or in his cot for longer than normal, I started to ignore his cry and let him get hysterical before I would even register it and by that point, I was too frustrated to see to him. I began to start thinking that he did not deserve a feed and to have his nappy changed because all he had done is cause distress since the day he was conceived. I eventually became completely withdrawn from him and shamefully I would not touch him or even look at him. The resentment and anger grew and grew. I was aware I was neglecting him, but I had no plans to change this.

Then the negative thoughts kicked in, as well as every other negative emotion. I became terrified of judgement from the outside world. I believed the house was being watched twenty-four hours a day by social workers; they were lined up outside my window watching the house, and all my neighbours were working undercover for social services. On the rare occasion I did go outside, I felt that everyone was watching me and following me; anyone on the phone was reporting back to social services. I knew they were going to take my children. The fear wasn't that they were going to take the baby, because that's what I wanted. The fear was that they were going to take my daughter, the centre of my universe. It was so very real. I was in a very dark and scary place.

The paranoia grew, and I explored every possibility to make the baby disappear. Adoption? Leave him in the supermarket? Cot death? Every possibility went against my morals. So the only way out was to take my own life. That was the best option, that would cause the least amount of heartache. I thought of hundreds of different ways I could do it, and finally came to the agreement with myself that I was going to book a hotel where no one would ever find me and take all the pills I needed to successfully end my life. I still hadn't told a soul anything; my loved ones knew I was low, but they had no idea of the extent. The night I had planned to do it, I waited till everyone was in bed fast asleep, and I climbed into bed with my daughter to say my goodbyes. I whispered to her, as I stroked her hair, to never forget me, that this is not her fault and that I would always be with her and love her forever. At that moment she woke up and gave me a cuddle and said: "I love you mummy". I suddenly snapped out of this dark mindset and knew that she needed me and I couldn't leave her. She saved me.

The next morning when my husband woke, I told him everything. He took me to the doctors and I found myself in a mother and baby mental health unit. They searched my bags and took a lot of my possessions; for my safety, they said. The first few days were horrible. When the risk to myself had lowered, I began to take back care of the baby, which was terrifying as I hadn't touched or looked at him for well over a week. My confidence slowly built and after a week I was doing basic care for him. My family came in almost every day, but I desperately missed my daughter. It was heart breaking saying goodbye to her every day and the blame and resentment toward the baby grew; it was his fault I was here and his fault that I was away from my beautiful daughter. I could see a glowing light around her, she could do no wrong, she was perfect in every way, and he was everything but.

Time moved very slowly in the unit, and the 'dark unspeakable' were still very present. I spoke to therapists and doctors daily and was diagnosed with adjustment disorder and severe postnatal depression. Around two weeks in, I demanded adoption papers from the doctor and wouldn't take no for an answer; it was my choice, I did not want this baby, I wanted to go home without him and go back to my beautiful family. I was told that I was not legally mentally stable to make that decision. The disappointment of not being able to make this decision was infuriating and the thoughts grew again as they always did. I could invent a time machine. I held onto this fantasy for a while until I told a nurse one day. She explained that if I was successful I would be a millionaire; my response was: you can have every penny, I just want to go back to my life before the baby. This became a strong possibility and I absolutely believed I could do it. When I finally realised this was just a fantasy and I wasn't clever enough anyway, my thoughts turned darker and I began to hope that the baby would pass away.

I spent six weeks in the unit. The bond with the baby was making slow progress and so was I. On the third day of being home I had a very real, gruesome nightmare that involved both my children and extremely horrific scenes. The next morning a metal health nurse came to visit and I told her every detail. I started having visions of the nightmares and at first, I kept them under control, but they quickly grew out of control. My breathing became extremely erratic, and I could not hear anything around me, I had slipped into a complete crisis. When I opened my eyes, I could see blood dripping from the ceiling and from my husband's face, so I kept my eyes tightly shut. I wasn't in control of my mind or body.

I made the decision I was going to jump in front of a train to end my life; the tracks sat conveniently at the end of our garden. I said goodbye to my husband and told him to find a woman who would make him happy and who would be good for my daughter. I told my mum to look after my beautiful girl and to take over the mother role. My biggest fear was always leaving my daughter, but I was going to be there in spirit if not in person. The illness had beaten me, I was too exhausted to fight it anymore. I knew it was my time to give up and my time to leave this life. The gruesome horrendous thoughts and the blood was still all around me, they were real. I knew that once I had gone, the blood would stop dripping, the knives and the glass would be put down and no one would get hurt. That was the only way I could make these unspeakable things stop.

My husband scooped me up and took me back to the mother and baby mental health unit. I blamed it all on the baby and once again completely withdrew from him. The next few weeks were hard work. I was exhausted and beaten by this dark cloud that had overtaken my mind. It was constantly throwing unspeakable thoughts around, and it was happy to have taken all of me. It had won.

I have never suffered from any mental health problems before, and if I'm completely honest I was a bit ignorant towards it. But I now know different; it is very real and very scary. I started making slow improvement and once again my confidence was slowly building towards the baby. After another three weeks I returned home again. I loved being around my daughter and spending every minute of the day with her. However, yet again my care with the baby stopped and I became completely withdrawn from him. Thoughts of ending my life were still very convincing and yet again I returned to the mother and baby mental health unit.

It has been nine weeks since I was admitted to a mental health hospital, and although I still haven't reached my happy ending, I am returning home again today to continue my recovery at home. With the right love and support I will get through to the brighter side. I am proud of myself and my family for all we have achieved together. Now, I am not ashamed of having a mental health illness. I will become the best mummy, wife, and daughter I can be one day soon.

October 2023 Update

I was given the diagnosis of postpartum psychosis not long after I wrote this back in 2019. Subsequently my medication and treatment were adjusted and I met a beautiful woman who was a peer support worker. She sat beside me one afternoon and began to tell me her story. She told me that just a few years ago she experienced postpartum psychosis and stayed in the same bed as me, in the same unit. Along with the treatment and peer support, my recovery began. The evil spirit began to dwindle, I started to face the baby, with support and lots of encouragement, I slowly took over his care and my mind began to repair. I remained in the mother and baby unit for a further three weeks, being there for ten weeks in total.

My mum brought me a soap making kit, mainly to pass the time but also to find something to take the focus away from the darkness and to spark some creativity back into me. Turned out I loved it and soap making helped me massively on my road to recovery. When I finally left the unit a week before Christmas, one of the lovely nurses suggested that I sell my soap and when I felt strong enough, share my story to help others. This is exactly what I did and Soap and Hope was born! With some time and lots of love, care, and soap making, I began to embark on the road to recovery; slowly my mind allowed me to take control again. Recovery wasn't easy, it was a rollercoaster and obviously Covid played a huge part in that. I learned to love my baby and to care for him again as his mum. With lots of therapy I learned that this wasn't his fault or mine - it was an illness.

When it was time to return to my midwifery degree, I decided I wasn't ready as it was highly possible that my psychosis could be triggered by being around pregnancy and birth. But it was clear that I had a new path laid out for me. I wanted to share my story to raise awareness, stop the stigma and bring hope to others who were suffering.

I now work as a family support worker, supporting families with their mental health and I use my lived experience to help others. I also share my story though Soap and Hope and in the media. I have so much support around me and am currently having therapy to process the trauma of this horrible illness.

I adore both my children, equally. They are simply amazing. My husband is my rock and my best friend, and we are stronger than ever. My Mum is my world and since I have recovered she has begun working for the NHS as a carer/peer support worker for families who are supporting someone with psychosis. I am so proud of her.

My son and I have made up for every moment we lost out on - in abundance! He has just started school and is my best mate (his words!) and my daughter is as amazing as ever. I am forever thankful to my wonderful family, friends and professionals involved in my care.

https://www.soapandhope.co.uk
On this website there is also a link to find support and a list of useful contacts.

Email Lacey at: Soapandhope1@outlook.com

https://www.nhs.uk/mental-health/conditions/post-partum-psychosis

Judi Burke

Judi is a woman with a beautiful and 'elegant' heart which is apparent in her very essence which shines from deep within. The challenge of life-threatening illness and traumatic surgery severely tested her courage but with her daughter's unfailing care and her deep faith, Judi became accepting, then calm and unafraid. Choosing to learn from her experiences, to come to a place of acceptance, and to use her learnings to help others, has given Judi great peace.

For every ailment under the sun
There is a remedy or there is none
If there be one, try to find it;
If there be none, never mind it.

(Mother Goose. 1695)

I have chosen to begin my story with a 17th century saying because as I grow older – but not necessarily wiser – I realise that an understanding of acceptance is the key to a life infused with contentment, something which is sought by many but experienced by few.

When I was approached by Susie to submit my story, I was reluctant to do so. Yes, I had experienced some very challenging times but I didn't honestly feel that they merited inclusion in her book 'Women of Spirit'. With further reflection however, I decided to write about what I had been through with the hope and intention that my story might interest and galvanise readers to find an inner strength they might not be aware they possess.

I lived in India for sixteen years, the first seven with my husband and the last nine as a single mother. I had arrived in 1997 with my four-year old son, nineteen-month old daughter and five months pregnant with my third child. I was joining my (half-Jamaican) husband who had gone out to start a consultancy business two months prior to our arrival. It was an interesting and challenging experience to live and make our way as a mixed-race couple/family in a deeply conservative country and society. Notwithstanding initial difficulties, we adapted and settled down very quickly, especially after I had given birth to our son, Noah in Bombay. The children joined local schools, made lots of friends and learnt to speak Hindi and a smattering of Marathi. Within two years, I set up my own business – a corporate training consultancy and was delivering workshops in various major cities around India. Working with so many different groups of men and women as well as bringing up three children in this fascinating country gave me a huge insight into and understanding of the Indian psyche.

After my husband and I separated I made the decision to stay on in

India whilst he returned to the UK. Life was extremely challenging as a foreign, single mother but despite many hardships and difficulties, I was determined to make my way and be happy in India, a country I had come to love and respect deeply. And then came the bombshell.

I had always been blessed with very good health and felt very young for my age. I was lucky enough to have had three easy pregnancies with normal, if rather long deliveries, but otherwise I had never been hospitalised for anything major in my life. Then, one Saturday afternoon, after a week of having moved house on the Monday and delivering three days of training, I experienced very bad haemorrhaging and was immediately admitted to our local hospital. After a barrage of invasive tests the following day; colonoscopy, CT and MRI scans, I was diagnosed with rectal cancer and told I needed surgery to remove the tumour. That was the bad news. The good news was that the cancer was in its early stages and didn't appear to have spread to other organs in my body.

Throughout this traumatic couple of days, I was supported by loyal friends who had driven me to the hospital, my seventeen-year old daughter Caitlin and my boyfriend. Other good friends also came to be with me during tests and results but it was my teenage daughter who was constantly by my side, giving me strength and courage to face what was coming. I called my various family members in the UK, including my two sons who were by then living with their father, to give them the news and each conversation was a very difficult and emotional one, as you can probably imagine.

Despite my shock at the situation in which I found myself, I realised that this was the time for me to accept the test results but also retain my sense of humour and put things in perspective, as far as possible, given the situation. The surgeon and medical staff were helpful, respectful and polite but not used to experiencing a patient with a sense of humour!

My surgery was scheduled for six days later as my surgeon wanted me to have time to organise for family members to come to India from the UK but I decided, together with my daughter, that this wouldn't be necessary as we had enough support from wonderful friends in India.

In the days preceding the surgery, I was able to draw strength and courage from my Buddhist faith; I chanted fervently and felt incredibly strong and uplifted by the amount of love and support I received from dear friends who visited me and the knowledge that everyone, especially my fellow SGI Buddhist members, was remembering me when they chanted and prayed. My Buddhist group leaders all told me that on the morning of the surgery, everyone would be chanting for me throughout the operation. For this reason, I was truly unafraid. I felt a kind of serenity and absolute certainty that the procedure would go well and that my surgeon would successfully remove the tumour and any surrounding cancerous cells.

To cut a very long story short, the surgery was, indeed a success but unfortunately, my recovery had severe problems due to my main abdominal incision failing to heal properly and gradually opening up into a big hole, very close to the stoma that fed into my ileostomy bag.

I look back on this period and realise that it was a far greater trial for my daughter than for me as it is sometimes easier to be the patient rather than a family member caring for the patient. I freely admit that I wasn't very brave when it came to handling the pain and discomfort of my wound being cleaned and dressed daily or the weekly event of my ileostomy bag being changed. My daughter had absolutely no prior nursing experience but after being shown what to do only once by a senior nurse at the hospital, she took over complete responsibility for my day-to-day nursing care at home in-between frequent check-ups with my surgeon. In India, there are no district nurses who make home visits after a surgery and I was told, in no uncertain terms, that my daughter's care would far surpass that of any private agency nurse I might care to employ! One of my oldest friends (and a fellow Buddhist) would often come and chant with me in the evenings and actually 'chanted me through' my terrible fear of the pain of my dressing being changed. It kept me going when all else seemed to fail.

I will never really understand what kept my daughter so strong through all of this. She demonstrated inner reserves of strength, calm and determination that totally defied her tender years. She nursed me through the entire recovery period before the second surgery six weeks later to reverse the ileostomy and was literally by my side, night and day from the time I was first admitted until it was all over and we triumphantly boarded our flight to London to go home for Christmas on 14th December, three weeks after my second surgery.

It was a strange and difficult time for both of us, not least because our roles were reversed as she became the mother and I, the child. I often felt resentment instead of pride and wonder at the way she controlled the complete situation. I felt lost and out of my comfort zone of parenting and this led to frequent emotional outbursts from both sides. Those weeks of illness and slow, painful recovery were a strain almost beyond endurance for both of us and yet, we came through it together, bound by an intensity of co-dependence and fear, anger and love, trust and friendship.

I finally began to comprehend what it meant to accept any given situation, however challenging, and detach myself from it in order to live through it and come out the other side with a sense of gratitude and wonder.

There are so many theories about life-threatening illnesses, for example cancer, and why people are presented with these terrible conditions. I have my own thoughts about the subject and what I have now come to a fuller understanding of, is this: everything in our lives is happening as it should; all the major experiences we go through - especially the bad ones – are potential opportunities for great learning. The important thing is to *make* the learning and to transform our lives and, I believe, our karmas through our learning.

Nichiren Daishonin's Buddhism, the Buddhist philosophy I follow, is helping me to do just that and for this reason, I can honestly say that I am grateful for having had the experience of my cancer as it has given me such a huge opportunity to alter my karma and bring about a fundamental personal change. It brought me much closer to my daughter and made me realise what is truly important in life: first to understand that it is vital to show compassion to ourselves so that we can then learn to show compassion to others and second, to make a positive difference to others' lives.

And so, what does one do with this whole experience and how does one go forward 'walking the talk'?

During the year following my cancer diagnosis, two surgeries and recovery, I qualified as a yoga teacher and then decided that after sixteen years of life in India, it was time to relocate back to the UK to look after my ageing mother and to do some 'giving back'. I knew that it would be a challenge for me to leave my beloved India, my daughter, who chose to stay and work first in Delhi and then Mumbai, all my old and very dear friends and my work there but I was keenly aware that one era of my life was coming to an end and a new one was beginning.

I had a strong vision that once back in the UK, I wanted to make a positive difference to others through teaching medical yoga to alleviate stress and help those with debilitating illnesses. My plans for this were, however, about to be derailed by further health problems and surgeries – a direct result of my original abdominal wound's failure to close properly.

Thus, it has been yet another interesting learning for me to accept that teaching yoga is no longer feasible for the foreseeable future, if at all, and so I have decided to research other avenues to help others with mental and physical health issues through mindfulness, meditation and pranayama workshops. It is a work in progress, as the saying goes. In the meantime, I continue to deliver corporate training to clients in Asia whenever I am offered assignments and am always guided in all that I do by the Buddhist teaching I follow: to make a positive difference to all those with whom I come into contact.

Biography

I was born in Stockholm, Sweden and spent the first five years of my life there before moving to the UK. As formal education doesn't begin until the age of seven in Sweden, I attended quite a few pre-school art/craft, dance and play groups and was always literally one step behind, trying to understand what was going on due to my lack of proficiency in Swedish. This struck a chord… once we moved to the UK, I was lucky enough to grow up in the beautiful countryside of Kent, schooling locally and then went to Edinburgh university to read modern European languages.

After graduation, I worked in public relations then advertising, followed by export sales/marketing before moving into the field of learning and development through educational and then corporate training, first in the UK and then in India and the Far East. My passion became cross-cultural sensitisation and understanding as I experienced the difficulties arising from people's misunderstanding of each other. The common thread running through my professional life has always been communication – both written and spoken, in English and other languages.

Until recently I specialised in all forms of communication skills training, cross-cultural sensitisation, values and ethics, performance management, change management, team building and leadership, time management and personal effectiveness and last but not least, through my company for stress management and wellbeing through yoga and mindfulness.

As the years have passed, I have realised that my passion for communication and listening is intrinsic to who I am and what I have done. Communication is what links and binds people. It is what brings people together who might otherwise experience antipathy due to lack of understanding and even worse, suspicion and fear.

My Buddhist faith and practise plays a huge part in my life because it is through the Soka Gakkai International (SGI) Buddhist practise that I have been not only able to cope with life's challenges but to welcome them as opportunities for spiritual growth and development.

For more information on SGI Buddhism, please go to www.sgi-uk.org

Jenna Harwin

Not everyone who has suffered sexual abuse as a child and been let down by so many in the system – and for so long – stays strong enough to become a teenage parent and find such deep love for her daughter. This unconditional love and knowing that she had a job to do – to protect her daughter, has enabled both Jenna and her two daughters to develop into strong, independent, resilient and oh-so-brave women.

A woman I was, even before I was a child. The reasons for this are unclear. It takes a lot to hold on to one's insecurities, to feel them, live and breathe them. I have learnt to live with and celebrate them and use them as a source of strength in everything I do. My story is dedicated to the strength, courage, and resilience of all women but especially my two wonderful daughters.

My father, when with us – he died when I was 17, covered-up life's troubles with his dry sense of humour. Going into my teens his humour frustrated me. He was no longer funny. The me today that has lived a whole lifetime without my dad, would give anything to hear his voice and even that dry sense of humour of his, although I suspect I would still not find him all that funny! For me, he was the very essence of what a man should embody. He always protected his family, although his methods didn't always make sense to me. I had him on a pedestal, I his princess and he my hero. Like with most parents, they eventually fall from that pedestal and are seen for all their imperfections, all that they are – human. This unfortunately happened for me not long before my dad died. I never did get to tell him how much I loved him. I hope he knew.

My parents, despite getting divorced when I was five, had a unique and caring relationship. My dad was always there for my mum and despite their many differences, they remained as a family. It wasn't perfect, nothing ever is. Witnessing my hero, my dad as a much older man protecting his family and doing so, so selflessly, is where my story begins. His unconditional love for everyone around him was admirable. I didn't see it then, but I do now. I wanted to love just as hard as he did and always be the person who fights for my family. As I write this, I realise this is still present tense for me, I want to make a difference and be that unconditional source of strength for those around me. For most of my adult life, I wasn't rescuing myself – I wasn't kind to myself, I didn't set boundaries. Today, I am much healthier and have negotiated a way of being just like him as much for my family as I show up for me too.

My mum is a young mother. As a child, I remember her as a single woman, dancing, smiling with a zest for life that was infectious. My mum has faced overwhelming challenges including loss and grief. She hid this well. I remember my mum started crying, crying a lot and it feels as though the tears haven't stopped, not since her thirty-eighth birthday. I remember feeling that I needed to make it better, whatever 'it' was. This was one of my first opportunities not that it was a conscious thought, but nonetheless for me to be that selfless source of strength I had learnt from my dad. I love my mum and I loved my dad and I love that between them, through their imperfections, they've made me who I am today. They did the best they could. That's all any of us can do. In my early twenties, a counsellor told me that I hadn't had a good childhood. This angered me. This is not my truth. I had an amazing childhood. I felt loved. Is that not the very essence of a good childhood? My truth is… my childhood was full of laughter, fun, curiosity, adventure, and love. I also experienced pain, hurt and heartbreak. Yet my childhood was still a good one.

During those 'happyish' times with my young energetic mum and 'sometimes' funny dad my innocence was being stolen. Stolen by a man who just so happened to be a part of that very family that reinforced my 'ideals' of love, belonginess and hope. An adult male cousin. This man today, still walks free, 'innocent'. His name, K. K would watch Barney, the purple dinosaur with me on repeat – this made me feel safe. At aged six, Barney was my comfort blanket. The songs about family and togetherness always stayed with me. So much so I sing them with my own children… 'mummy loves you, you love mummy…'. When this man would subject me to repeated episodes of abuse, when he would touch me, I would always think of Barney. I couldn't tell those closest to me, not without hurting them. Not without falling short of being that source of strength that I so desperately wanted to be. I didn't understand what was happening to me and just how wrong it was. I would pretend to be asleep during the abuse. I was numb to the pain, not consciously aware of the pain I was feeling, even though I was awake.

This was how I coped.

Back then, I told my cousin of a similar age what was happening to me. We were both so young. She told me she was also being abused by the same man. Suddenly, I didn't feel alone, but it did normalise what was happening somewhat. Together, we eventually told her mum, my aunty. This made sense to me as it kept distance between my closest family (those I wanted to protect) and what was happening to us. Maybe I could protect them and stop K from harming us, all at the same time. Either way, it was no longer just about me, I had to protect my cousin. This is what I do – I have always protected others. Some say this is a trauma response. They may be right, but for me it has been who I am for as long as I can remember and has both served and harmed me. The abuse eventually stopped, but everything else continued as normal. Why was K not being punished? Why did no one acknowledge what had happened? Why has he still not been punished?

As I grew older, I hated him, I hated being around him, I felt angry with him. I'm not sure I understood why, and I didn't consciously allow myself to remember why. Aged fourteen, I told my mum. She and I went to the police. The system let me down. The aunty we had told as children denied us ever reporting the abuse to her. As fragile as my mum was, she stood by me and gave me the strength I needed to stand up and be counted. This was the first time I truly allowed myself to be heard. I showed myself kindness and trusted myself that I could do the right thing. My wider family, those who knew and are closely related to K disowned me and to this day continue to protect K. It used to hurt. It doesn't anymore. I pity them. It is not my shame, it is theirs.

At the age of thirteen, I was living with my dad in a bed and breakfast waiting for our forever home. My mum had remarried and had two more children. I was unhappy, lonely, and uncertain about almost everything; typical adolescent challenges, but I was also feeling a painful distance between me and those I loved most. It was at this time a twenty-two-year-old man groomed me and my family. Of course, I didn't see this for what it was back then. I was lost and confused.

It wasn't long before I felt hopeful again. I had thought about not using his name – for so long saying it allowed caused an unbearable lump in my throat. My story is my truth, and I will say his name as I type just the initial - that is within my power. His name: B. B tapped into my feelings of maturity, of being a woman before my time. He made me feel understood, recognised, and he was the only one who looked at me and saw my pain. It was the summer of 2003; I was thirteen years old. It was like a film. B would take me out in his car, he bought me gifts and shared his story. Amazingly, he had a similar story to mine. One of secrecy, loss, abuse and fear. He met a need that at the time no one seemed to be meeting. I believed he had my best intentions at heart. He insisted we had to keep our 'friendship' a secret as no one would understand. This was no problem for me, I had a kept a similar secret for several years to protect my family and this was no different. B groomed, sexually abused, and violated me. I didn't know then what grooming was or the impact it would leave on my life. These people are charming and appear honest, and loyal. They hide in plain sight. I couldn't escape. I didn't know how to escape.

The police became involved, Children's Services, the Criminal Justice System, and the school throughout the five years that the abuse continued. The system let me down. They let my family down. Their messaging was conflicting. Certain professionals were quite threatening, abrupt, and judgemental. Aged fourteen and heavily pregnant, I was told by my health visitor whilst I stood, so tired, in my family kitchen that I would not emotionally bond with my child. This sweeping statement has had huge implications for me as a mother and as a woman. At the age of fifteen I gave birth to my daughter. All that unconditional love I had shared growing up, that source of strength I wanted so desperately to be, the woman I was… all this suddenly had a home. That wave of love and need to protect as a parent is wonderful but equally at times can feel suffocating. I knew from the moment I held her that I had a job to do. I had to protect my baby. Today, she is eighteen and is at university. I am so proud of her. As a mother, I have made many mistakes and have many regrets. This is part of being a parent, I guess. I have held on tightly, very tightly. My aim, to break the intergenerational cycle that has haunted our family. My girls are so strong, always speak out and set boundaries for themselves. My story, although full of pain, is one of survival. A story that makes me a better mother, a better woman and human every day.

I find myself growing younger as I grow older. I am strong, independent, and resilient. I have learned to live through and within a system that continues to let us down. Knowing that each day, I and my girls continue to grow and make good choices is what carries me through. We may not have all the answers and nowhere near enough justice, but what we do have is something that is real. We will always rise above adversity and do better than we have before. This sets us aside from those people who choose to hurt others and steal from them something so precious: innocence. Those people are not open to growth and a realisation of who they are. We will not be defeated. They are small people, and they miss out on those things that really matter - never will they experience true, unconditional love. And with that, I and my girls challenge ourselves to change our world every day.

I dedicate my story to all the brave, wonderful, resilient women, and mothers; you are doing amazingly well and will continue to flourish *in spite of* adversity.

Biography

Jenna Harwin was born in Norfolk in 1990. With a strong curiosity and a drive to challenge the world around her, she continues her journey of affecting change. In 2016, she graduated from the University of Suffolk with a Sociological based Master of Arts degree. Stimulated by its philosophical underpinnings, she later enjoyed studying her PhD researching intergenerational resilience among mothers and their daughters. She has had a varied career including volunteering in Southeast Asia, empowering women and children to perceive of themselves as leaders. Working with the non-for-profit sector before moving into the leadership and development space, Jenna found her passion for individual and executive coaching.

Currently working in local government, she manages projects provoking improved outcomes for her local community. Jenna is a thriving coach working with many clients including topics such as confidence, leadership skills, relationships, and transformational change. She has a keen interest in the origins and development of resilience living each day in much the same way, with feedback from her clients fuelling her passion for supporting others in their journey of self-discovery.

Jenna lives in Norfolk where she raises her two daughters, enjoying the serenity of the surrounding forest and spending time with her children and many animals (including a ferret!). She hopes the sharing of her story will contribute towards a shared movement – for those women and children who have ever felt let down by the system, scared, uncertain or alone. To remind us all, to celebrate triumphs no matter how small, as one step forward in a world that can be unkind and unjust is always a win!

linkedin.com/in/jenna-harwin-ma-pg-dip-pg-cert-802b87ab
jenna.harwin17@gmail.com

Gabriella Guglielminotti Trivel

A sparkling Italian, Gabriella loved adventure. Marrying young, the fairy-tale relationship became more and more distorted, daily events becoming opportunities for her husband to highlight her inadequacies and need to be 'supervised'. Self-discovery was embraced after divorce with training in Neuro Linguistic Programming, and the adventurous Gabriella was set free to travel the Antarctic – the beginning of more adventures!

Melt down in Antarctica!

I left my country because I wanted to join the man I loved and was thirsty for adventure. I wanted new horizons, so I left Turin in Italy and moved to London in the United Kingdom. Changing country, language and culture does stretch you enormously, even if you are an adventurer at heart like me. It is good in a way that one can't see all the difficulties ahead at the outset and just find out step by step on the way, otherwise one would never move.

In 1998, I took the leap and full of enthusiasm, I started my new life in the UK that I had dreamt of for so long. The previous year I met a British man while I was working in the Maldives as a tour operator and fell in love with him.

I enjoyed the first phase of my English life tremendously, even if it was very tiring, as I like new beginnings. I like having to adjust to a different environment, question my beliefs and habits, as it makes me feel alive. I liked the challenge of the language too; even though I had studied English for eight years before moving to the UK and had qualified as an interpreter, I was tested big time when I moved to London. Living in such a big cosmopolitan capital with so many accents to cope with was an enormous effort.

Then there was the challenge of learning to live with a man of a different culture and, even though love smooths many edges and corners, sometimes it can be hard beyond belief.

Of course, to find work and then learn how to survive in the work environment was another interesting part of my life in the UK. My plate was full, but my heart was happy and felt very much alive, what more could I ask for? Years flew by, and I was busy with so many new things, challenges, personal issues, and family problems.

At some point, I started noticing that my nature wasn't as sparkling as it used to be; from time to time I would feel worried and anguished and would catch myself toying with not so positive thoughts and even focusing on death. I must have repressed this for some time before I became aware of it. When I started noticing it, I felt shocked and scared. I asked myself: "What is this all about?" I had never had thoughts like that, even in my life's darkest moments, and I had experienced some tough times for sure when I was still living in Italy. These thoughts grew with time and my concern grew as well, but I didn't know what to do about it.

Even if my relationship with my British man wasn't satisfying, I had agreed after all to get married! I was definitely under the spell of the new country, relationship, life, work, friends, etc. Getting married was a new adventure for me, so why not embark on it?

Yes, bring it on, I love it!

The fact that I was proposed to in an exotic location on holiday made up for the fact that our relationship had huge problems, as there was too much 'baggage' on both sides. I decided to follow my heart and go for it anyway, rather than evaluating what was already there to be considered carefully. The romantic wave got the better of me and I slipped quickly along the slippery slope called 'the romantic adventure'. I didn't pay much attention, in the heat of the moment, to my conditioning and limited experience of life, even if I had already travelled extensively and had previous relationships under my belt. The allure of getting married to a man that I deemed to be interesting and exciting took over and all wisdom and common sense was silenced and put to sleep. Of course, I was following my heart, but back then I didn't know that the most important thing in life is actually to know oneself well enough, so to be able to be an observer and allowing oneself to see everything without censoring too much. I had censored for years all those bits that I didn't like, because I wanted my 'romantic dream' to be true at all costs, even when all the hints and facts were showing me the opposite. Little Gabriella was impressed to have conquered the heart of a man, rather than knowing the depths of her own heart: the only one to be conquered.

After the adventure of getting married, which kept me busy for several months, things got worse and worse and I had to start facing situations that I never wanted to deal with and had put up with for years to be able to keep cherishing my dream.

Life finds a way to talk to you and wake you up, even when you play deaf, dumb and blind. The blows got bigger and more painful so that I would pay attention and couldn't ignore them anymore. My heart started talking to me so loudly that I had to listen, and I found myself in a very sore spot. Happy normal conversations gave way to numerous discussions that became abusive, and verbal fights where the only way out was shutting up. Any daily event would become an opportunity for my husband to highlight my inadequacies and need to be supervised. My needs would become second to his and belittled. What felt like support in the past became an insidious way to remind me that I couldn't possibly aim for what I wanted. What came across to me was that I wasn't good enough or qualified enough to be in a position to aim high, either in my working life or in any other areas.

Slowly but steadily I became a nice object for him to boast about, rather than a partner in his life; I was the trophy wife. Our intimate life became non- existent and I found myself regularly facing the question "Shall I find myself a lover?".

I didn't know back then that the love I had experienced in the beginning and which pushed me to move to the UK had become distorted. What I was experiencing was pure control by my husband rather than love, real, unconditional love. I knew that ignoring one's welfare and compromising are not conducive to anything good and lasting, especially in relationships. I knew that respect is paramount, otherwise everything else fails quickly and inexorably. Because I was playing deaf, dumb and blind, I had to learn the hard way.

At a certain point, everything in my life collapsed: my marriage, my work and my social background, connected mainly to my husband, all disappeared overnight. I felt destroyed, alone, aimless and hopeless. I didn't know any more where I was going and what I wanted. Even wanting something requires a bit of sense of self and self-consciousness and at that point I felt numb and stressed beyond measure. Feeling the pain and discomfort surprisingly, after a while, made me feel alive.

To escape from this situation, I had to listen to my heart, no more illusions of the mind and social conditioning, but simply listening to my body and soul. Within time I started remembering my desires and dreams of when I was a child and realised that they weren't really corresponding to where I was and what I had achieved so far. Something might have gone wrong along the way I thought.

Slowly I realised that I had always considered myself powerful and strong, but I wasn't any longer, so what had I lost on the way? Where had my certainty gone? My desires? My dreams and my joy of life? I became aware that getting out of that situation might take some time and effort, maybe as much time and effort as it took to get there.

When my husband decided to file for divorce, I said yes to his big surprise, and started saying yes to anything that would come up from the depths of my soul: yes, yes, yes!

I went back on my path of self-discovery that started when I was in my twenties and decided to train in Neuro Linguistic Programming. I started reading books again about personal development like 'The Power of Now' by Eckhart Tolle and others. I travelled on my own with a backpack through Vietnam for a month.

I realised that Gabriella was cool and there was no reason to be ashamed of myself, I was actually a wonderful woman. I decided that in the future I wouldn't allow anybody to tell me who I am and try to change me. As a consequence of this I wouldn't try to change anybody else either. I understood that I can't change anybody, except myself. Realising that felt good and very freeing. I was free and happy to be me again.

The period of going through the divorce process was long and really tested my inner strength. I had many low points and it felt never ending. I knew though that it would end one day and with my new awareness I would be stronger and more marvellous than ever before. It was a period of reflection, work on myself, cleansing and purging from the depths of my soul and listening attentively to what my heart had to say. Soon after the legal process had ended, I came across the opportunity to join an expedition to Antarctica and this time, as crazy as it might sound, it was easy for me to listen to my heart and say yes. Deep in my heart I knew that I had waited for something like this all my life and now it was time to let go of my fears, limiting beliefs and doubts, and just listen to my soul which was hungry for adventure. What better opportunity than joining a group of people going to Antarctica to face fears and limiting beliefs?

I felt super alive, life's heartbeat was synchronised with mine and I felt one with little Gabriella again. Little Gabriella was that part of me that hadn't been loved, listened to, nurtured and respected enough, because it was wild and untameable and certainly not complying with societal rules and standards, family expectations or other people's opinion of what is right or wrong. I felt cherished and heard again. I could feel my confidence growing and my joy for life coming back to me, what a wonderful feeling!

The nine months preceding my departure for the Antarctic continent were of preparation and introspection. Why was I going there? What was my spirit searching for? What did I want next in my life? The questions were many and my mind was driving me mad at times.

I kept cleansing my body, being active and fit, dealing with my inner issues and looking forward to facing the unknown. After a few months of pondering I came to the conclusion that facing the unknown was what I had set myself up for and all my worries and questions crowding my mind were the result of that, nothing more, nothing less.

Ultimately the 'Fear of the Unknown' is generally what is behind any specific fear we face on a daily basis.

I know, being a certified Master Practitioner of Neuro Linguistic Programming, that fear is the acronym of: False Experience Appearing Real. I know that fear is mainly in the mind, as very rarely in this day and age, we face the fear of being attacked by a lion or being bitten by a poisonous snake, unless of course we live in a wild environment, but that wasn't my case. I knew that feeling anxious and uncertain about going to Antarctica was triggering all my unsolved issues, uncertainties, beliefs. The fact that I had to deal with those fears for nine months, before physically leaving for the expedition, made it all worse and more difficult: a real test of endurance even before departure.

At times, mental resilience can be as challenging as physical resilience. I realised that I had to put myself in another sore spot, but this time my heart was leading me towards my destiny and it was my conscious choice! When I was about a month away from my departure, my heart knocked on my door and asked for an audience. I opened the door and paid attention to what was there for me to listen to. I needed to do something while I would be in Antarctica to record my experience, so that it could be available for other people too. I wasn't going there just for pleasure or seeing the penguins in the flesh, I was going there to grow, contribute to myself and others and ultimately leave a legacy.

"What are you going to do about it?" I heard my heart asking. My mind went blank, I couldn't find an answer other than: "Well, I will keep a diary during my trip, so that I can record my thoughts, experiences and…" I realised quite quickly that writing a diary wouldn't be enough, so what else could I do? I could film, that's it! In fact, I had enjoyed and grew so much as a result of watching documentaries, why couldn't I do that? Good idea in principle, but I didn't have enough funds to pay for a cameraman to come with me to Antarctica, therefore what else could I do?

It became quite clear to me that the only thing I could do was filming the adventure myself, as this would minimise my costs, but I had never filmed before in my life. Help!

"Well you will just do it" my heart said and then there was silence, no more words.

There we go again: a new thing to deal with and unravel, oh joy. I knew that I couldn't turn a deaf ear to this, so I might as well just go and look for help about cameras, camcorders and filming. I soon found myself with support to acquire the information and equipment I needed. I was happy. Metaphorically I was on top of a mountain admiring the wonderful landscape and I hadn't even left for Antarctica yet!

What happened next was unforeseeable and tested me beyond my expectations.

I managed to leave for my big trip with some basic photographic gear to be able to take good pictures and film the main activities that I would engage in with the group of people who were coming with me. I felt happy and ready for the challenge, but what happened on the first day as we set foot on the Antarctic continent was spectacular, extraordinary, mind blowing and above all inescapable.

While we were climbing an ice wall near the shore, I left my photographic gear in my rucksack on the rocky beach, as I had never climbed ice before and didn't want to be burdened with things I didn't need. I thought I would film the climb the next time I did it, once I had acquired a little more skill. I had gone up the wall and come down and was about to secure my buddy to do the same when I looked out at sea and saw a huge iceberg on the other side of the bay start moving, calving and then collapsing into the sea!

It all happened in slow motion as I had seen in documentaries.

I forgot about myself and just became at one with this extraordinary experience: I could barely talk but then managed to shout to the others "Look!"

Before I knew it a huge wave, formed by the motion of such a huge amount of ice, reached the little beach where we had left all our things and flooded it completely.

I was harnessed to the ice wall and had crampons on my feet, so there was no way I could have freed myself quick enough to run after my rucksack before the waves reached the shore.

I witnessed the demise of my filming project in a blink of an eye and could do nothing to save it! My full story is told in detail in my book 'Antarctic Odyssey, a New Beginning'. In my book, I share the part of the ice which is below the surface: my inner journey.

After ten days in the Antarctic peninsula with the group on the ship, I went off travelling on my own around Patagonia, Chile, and Easter Island before going back to London. When I arrived back home, I realised that I didn't fit in the box of the 'old me' any longer. So, what was I to do now? I couldn't go back and try to have a so called 'normal life' simply because I wasn't normal any more.

I had stretched myself beyond belief, so now I couldn't just go back to be the 'old me' and feel happy with it, it just wasn't possible. It would be like trying to wear a pair of shoes that are one size smaller than your feet, it would be extremely uncomfortable and not really possible.

What was next for me after having gone to the freezer of the Earth? The only place I could think of that would stretch me further would be going to Mars or outer space, but that would be tricky to put into action. After a bit more soul searching I realised that I had challenged myself all my life and it wasn't necessarily going to a more remote place that would make me grow and progress after what I had already done. Maybe there were challenges that I had ignored that were waiting for my attention and some resolution closer to home. It was a time of real reflection again, being honest with myself and get ready for big changes. I felt anxious and restless, unsatisfied, and looking for peace, as I couldn't find it anywhere. This time though, I felt better equipped, as I had already been in that situation and I knew that the only way out was by listening to my heart. I let go and allowed myself to feel the despair, the low point after the exhilaration of feeling on top (or should that be the bottom) of the world.

My heart kept talking to me louder and louder and I could do only one thing and one thing only: listen to it and follow its orders. One morning in a moment of calm I realised that I had been calling myself a 'Flying Inspiration' for a few years and that I always wanted to learn to fly and become a pilot. Maybe learning to fly would be my next step on my journey of self-discovery. Surprise, surprise once we allow our heart to speak and we decide to follow it, the Universe conjures to help us against all odds!

Within a few days I was flying in a two-seater plane in the vicinity of where a few years earlier I had promised to myself, quietly in my heart, that one day I would be a pilot.

It took me a while to realise all this, as I was so taken by the experience of flying that I didn't notice. When I remembered though, I was speechless and had to surrender to the fact that I had to take action towards my dream. I couldn't just let it be, I had to move and take a leap of faith in that direction, even if I didn't know what the next step would be.

The more we open up to our heart and the more we follow its directions, the bigger the challenges are that show up in our life and the bigger the opportunities that are also presented to us. I knew that, but to experience it first hand, was another matter altogether.

Fears became bigger and bigger instead of disappearing from my life.

I thought I had had my initiation in Antarctica, I didn't know that was just the beginning!

Several months later while I was exploring the possibilities of learning to fly and become a pilot, I also came across Alexandra Pope and her work about the menstrual cycle.

I was intrigued by the subject, because during the last few years of my life by living dangerously and out of my comfort zone most of the time, my menstrual cycles became very erratic. I had expressed a desire in my heart to know more about it and asked the Universe to send me some information in this area. As the Universe always listens to us, my request was heard and delivered to me at the right time. I had read of a free conference call about the wisdom of menstruation with Alexandra Pope in an e-mail and decided to listen to it. A week later I also decided to go to her workshop.

Again, my heart was knocking on my door and once again I couldn't turn a deaf ear to it.

The moment I had waited all my life eventually arrived with lots of insights. It was like an avalanche, a whirlpool of energy flooding all my being and showed me a whole new universe: what an insightful moment! It was a 'Eureka' moment multiplied by ten. All of a sudden,

I was understanding so many things and, most important of all, I became aware of my life purpose!

A big turning point in my life was about to unfold with unforeseeable developments.

I realised that I wanted to empower women by helping them discover the wisdom of their body and their menstrual cycle. The moment I thought I would never experience was there for me in all its glory: "Oh my goodness, what next?" Well, there is only one thing that one can do in such moments: take action! I offered my support to Alexandra as I thought her message was so important. I organised few workshops with her and then I had to step up again, because my heart was calling me to play a bigger game. A year later I started holding my own workshops and developed my own work and message for women who want to grow and embrace their inner beauty.

I hope my story encourages you to look into your heart and listen to its directions. I can assure you that you will never be disappointed! May love and peace be with you at all times.

Biography

A 'Woman of the 21st Century', feminine cycle consultant Gabriella was born in Italy and studied foreign languages at the University of Turin, her home city. She is a qualified Master Practitioner of Neuro Linguistic Programming (NLP) and has travelled around Europe, Asia, Africa, America and Antarctica.

In 2012, she published her book, 'Antarctic Odyssey a New Beginning', about her adventures and collaborated with the book 'Note to Self: the Secret to becoming your own Best Friend' by Jo Macdonald.

In 2016, she collaborated with the book 'Reboot Your Life' with a chapter titled 'The Phoenix rises from the Ice in Antarctica'.

She is an author, speaker, visionary, and coach who helps women gain confidence, authority, and fulfilment in life by knowing their body. Details of all her services may be found on her website.

www.flyinginspiration.com

Dawn Swinley

A violent rape at the age of eighteen left Dawn feeling too traumatised to report it. So, for a long time she lived with her 'dirty secret', burying it deep to protect herself; becoming a control freak as a way of coping. Receiving unconditional love from her husband and family gave Dawn the strength to achieve success in her professional life. Finally, speaking openly about being raped has been not only a relief, but hugely empowering.

WHEN SUSIE INVITED ME TO BE part of her book, I really didn't feel as if I could contribute very much as a 'woman of spirit'; Susie disagreed and told me that my experience has made me the woman I am today and that telling my story could help many others.

I was raped, and I will say it again – I was raped. You may be asking yourself why did I do that? It has taken me years to really acknowledge and admit it, never mind talk about it. It was my dirty secret; I was only nineteen years old, very inexperienced and naïve as far as sex was concerned, having only lost my virginity to a long-standing boyfriend.

I was on college placement at a hotel in the Lake District having great fun and working hard. A group of us had been out, one of the girls had been talking with a couple of boys and they had come back with her to the staff block. I was in the wrong place at the wrong time, I certainly didn't ask for it but then no one does, woman, man, girl or boy!

I am not going to go into all the details except to say I didn't know him, he followed me when I left to go back to my room, it was very forceful and violent, it happened very quickly but it felt like a lifetime. Afterwards, he just got up and left, leaving me curled up on the floor crying. I remember running to the bathroom where I was physically sick and then I sat in a very hot bath and scrubbed myself raw, I drew blood. I was simply trying to wash it all away, telling myself it didn't happen. I sat in that bathroom for hours as I was so scared to leave thinking he may still be about. However, I did make it back to my room and I hid in the wardrobe, and I stayed there all night.

I kept asking myself why me, why me? What did I do to deserve that? I was scared but also angry, it felt unreal. I started going into denial, it didn't happen – that was my way of blocking it out. I was supposed to do a breakfast shift but I didn't, I got a friend to tell them I was sick. I stayed in my room all day curled up on the bed. I was bruised and very sore, I didn't want anyone to see me, I didn't want to answer any questions. I was hiding, hoping it would all go away. My friend eventually got me to open the door, she didn't ask me anything, she just hugged me. I think she knew, but no words were spoken. A couple of days passed and I felt brave enough to leave my room, I was still very sore; I hid my facial bruises with makeup, the others couldn't be seen.

To add insult to injury on a visit to the doctor a few weeks later I found out the rapist had given me Chlamydia. I was so upset and I felt dirty all over again. Luckily it was found in time and cleared up quite quickly but I had another dirty secret!

Time went on and it stayed my secret, I had buried it deep but it had left wounds. This man robbed me of my self-worth, he made me feel guilty, he ruined my feelings and attitude towards sex; my trust in men was destroyed. He took something that didn't belong to him, he had no right but he did it anyway.

I remember telling my elder brother about it a few years later, he was cross with me because I hadn't told him and I hadn't reported it but he promised not to say anything to anyone. I never said the word rape – I explained it as a sexual assault.

I wasn't going to let this control me so my life carried on, I passed my exams, I became airline cabin crew and saw the world, I secured good jobs and I met the man of my dreams and got married. We have just celebrated our twenty-first wedding anniversary.

I had had other boyfriends and I was engaged twice before I met my husband. Both of those men tried to control me in one way or another, tried to change me until I saw sense and ran in the opposite direction, I was lucky to escape from their clutches and needless to say my parents were overjoyed when the relationships were over. Neither of them really knew me as I know that I always held something back, a little piece of me. Maybe it's because I had a secret, I really don't know.

My mum is my best friend and before I married, I told her about the rape when the time felt right. She gave me the biggest hug and I know she would have done exactly the same if I'd told her when it happened and I would have had her support. She promised never to tell my dad, as I was his little girl and it was something he didn't need to know; he died eight years ago, never knowing. And I know that was the right decision.

My husband helped me heal completely; we've had a loving and happy relationship, he helped me trust again, he showed me how to love unconditionally and more importantly he helped me to love myself again. So, although I thought I had control, I didn't, well, certainly not emotionally.

Being raped came back to haunt me when we were trying for a baby; it just wasn't happening and I thought that having Chlamydia had made me infertile. That guilty, angry feeling overwhelmed me; it wasn't the case, but the stress and strain it put on our marriage was immense. We got through it together, and through IVF (a new procedure called ICSI – I'm sure my husband Casper enjoyed sticking needles in my butt every night for two weeks!) amazingly I got pregnant first cycle. Matt and Laura were born, five weeks premature, but perfectly healthy. I nearly died – but that's another story.

So, now a mum to two beautiful babies, I embraced the role and life carried on, and again the rape was filed and forgotten about.

When the twins we eighteen months old we moved from Cumbria back to my husband's family home in the Forest of Dean. I knew nobody and Casper worked away four nights per week, it was hard but like any northern girl I pulled up my sleeves, I joined nursery groups and I started making a new life for us. I was lucky to be a stay at home mum.

When Matt and Laura we about four years old I felt I needed to do something more than just being a mum, I wanted to give something back. I organised four successful charity balls over a period of five years, raising over £60,000 in total. I qualified in nutrition and set up my own business – and I am very passionate about this. However, there was something holding me back, I just didn't feel in control.

I had some counselling sessions and although I believed I had accepted the rape, I hadn't. I relived the attack, there was a lot of crying, but I had to release it so that I could finally move on and admit to myself that I was still holding on to the guilt, but it wasn't my fault.

A while later, and this may seem strange, but I did a parachute jump, raising money for my son who was going to Borneo on a World Challenge. I was extremely nervous, edging my way to the open door of the plane and for a split second I didn't feel in control – but I did feel safe as I was strapped to a hunky, trained ex-paratrooper. It was the most amazing experience, I felt free, and when my feet touched the ground I felt I had finally come to terms with being raped; it was all about not having control, and my emotions fell into place. I understood why some family and friends had often said to me I was a control freak, something I could never see, but it all led back to how that man made me feel so many years ago.

I am now fifty-three years of age and I'm writing about my experience. I have sat down and talked to my children about it; you see it's no longer a dirty secret, it's part of my life and part of me.

It's a conversation that I hope will help both my kids in different ways. Matt was very angry, while Laura was shocked that it had happened to her mum.

"No" means "No". Anyone can get raped; I've explained to the twins the importance of not getting totally drunk at parties, watching their drinks, not getting into bed with someone only to regret it the next day or to not know what happened the night before. They should be mindful of their surroundings and be aware that sex must be consensual..

I was raped and my only one regret is that I didn't report it to the police. Was I selfish? Possibly but at the time I just could not All I can do is pray that he didn't hurt anyone else.

Biography

Originally from Cumbria, I've lived in Gloucestershire for eighteen years. I am happily married to my husband Casper and have beautiful eighteen-year-old twins, Matt and Laura. Our family is complete with McKenzie, our ten-year- old Labrador and Lulu, six-year-old Westie.

A nutritional therapist known locally as 'The Drop a Dress Size Coach', I help women lose weight, balance hormones, increase energy whilst saving time and money, all through nutritional therapy and intolerance testing. Nutrition is my passion; I believe you are what you eat and that nutrition is about lifestyle changes, mindset, and moving your body. I hate the gym but I love walking the dogs every day. I also love travelling and exploring new places, and aim to do more of this one day.

www.dawnswinley.com
www.safeline.org.uk
www.thesurvivorstrust.org

Two

Failure is Not an Option

You can transcend all negativity
when you realise that the only power
it has over you is your belief in it.
As you experience this truth
about yourself you are set free.

Eileen Caddy

Sejal Payne

In September 1972, Idi Amin, a ruthless dictator, expelled almost all of Uganda's 50,000 Asians and seized their property. Sejal and her family were among the refugees who came to England with no money and just a few belongings, to begin a new and very different life in a culture so completely alien to their own. Sejal's delightfully warm personality has remained intact while tackling every challenge in her life – and there have been many – with calm determination and dignity.

IN 1972, WHEN I WAS TEN, my family came to England as refugees due to Idi Amin's expulsion of Asians. I remember that I had no passport, my birth hadn't been registered and I overheard conversations about what they would do if I couldn't travel with them. I remember being evacuated from school after shots had been heard at a nearby church, and later on discovering that a lot of black Christian boys had been shot. No one believed Idi Amin initially as the Indians had the core of the Ugandan economy, and when the realisation set in that he was serious, panic ensued. There were rumours of people going missing, being taken away and never coming back. At the airport that October, as we sat on the plane, my dad nearly didn't come with us. The Ugandan Army took him away as we were boarding and my poor mum had to sit on the plane, worrying about whether he would come back. He was lucky that he personally knew many of the army officers who used to frequent our shop and one of them recognised him and clarified the mistaken identity so he was allowed to leave and got to the plane just in time. What a different story our lives would have been if things had gone the other way.

In the United Kingdom, I found all the people and surroundings so different and exciting, but for my parents it was frightening; everything was taken out of their control. We lived in a refugee camp for a week, but those who could were encouraged to live with relatives, so we went to my cousins' home in Finchley. Sixteen people shared the top flat of a Victorian house; one bathroom and one kitchen, with a rota for using both. There was no talking about the situation – just coping.

My father had been an important man in the town in Uganda; an elder within the community and one of senior religious devotees in a then fast growing new branch of Hinduism – the Swaminarayan movement. He was a small business owner with no other skills, but had no money to set himself up in England, so never again owned his own business. I would say he lost an essence of himself because of this, but is not bitter. My mother's work had been to look after our extended family and she had never gone out to work. In the UK, my parents both ended up working in factories, where, because they were Indian, they weren't even allowed to eat their food in the canteen with everyone else, they had to sit outside.

My parents suffered a complete culture shock to their way of life; a disintegration of their community, and bringing up children in a culture that was so alien to them was hard for them to understand. They had no control over the things to which we children were being exposed. For my sisters and me, it was a constant battle; we were one person at home, totally another person outside, and none of the people we were with at either end appreciated what this was like. Mum and Dad had no idea of our difficulty; they obviously knew what we were being exposed to because they saw it in their daily life, but they were unable to help us deal with it and still strived to maintain our sense of culture, ethics and morals.

Dad was very strict, and until we were teenagers we respected him, then we started questioning things, which he found very hard. My mother was mediating all the time. She has been my inspiration in that she was very forward thinking, very creative, she liked learning about new things and encouraged us to do the same, and to make new friends. But at the same time, like my sisters and me, she was fighting a culture that was going against her own, very restricting culture. When we were teenagers we were the only Indian family I knew who welcomed English people into their home – boys or girls.

My parents had had an arranged marriage, and they wanted that for my sisters and me, but as teenagers, we didn't want Indian men because we were so negatively affected by our experiences – traditional life meant inequality to women. I definitely saw education as a way out, and with a lot of effort and struggle I found my niche. Hard work was ingrained in us from our parents; their work ethic comes from their history, change was difficult but they coped, they made the best of things and endeavoured to better themselves and wanted the same for us.

I left home to do nursing; my parents agreed to this provided I stayed in London and came home at weekends. I enrolled at Great Ormond Street, as I wanted to work with children. Co-incidentally, the lady who interviewed me had worked in Uganda, so straight away we clicked and she offered me a place. I met Simon in 1981; we were just friends for a long time, and my parents didn't know about our relationship until six years later. My father talked about me getting married, and asked if was I interested in a nice Indian doctor in Germany. I said that I wasn't! I was one of the first in our community to marry outside the Hindu faith. My parents didn't oppose the marriage but warned us that things might be very difficult for us, and that if we had children we must consider in which faith we would bring them up. Simon is Catholic but doesn't practice his religion so he is happy about the boys being classified as Hindus. I think my parents are very proud of us; all they want is for us to be happy. Interestingly enough there was more opposition from Simon's parents than from mine. However, the Indian community then and even now can still be judgemental; my parents caught the brunt of the backlash and gossip from their relatives and friends. Although nothing was actually ever said to me personally, it was felt. Now there is a more understanding relationship with the extended family as the British born Indian children are global citizens and issues as

mixed marriages are more common.

Living in Dubai, I felt for the first time that I was seen as only an Indian. Growing up in England I had come through all the cultural challenges but when I was nursing I never encountered discrimination. Dubai wasn't cosmopolitan then, it was rather segregated into ethnic communities: the expats, the Indians, Filipinos, Pakistanis, and Arabs. Apparently everyone in the English expat community knew that the next newcomer was married to an Indian, causing some wonderment. People would comment that I spoke English really well and asked me where I learned to speak it! It was apparent that although I saw myself as British other people didn't, and I'd never encountered that as an adult in England. There was curiosity about Simon and me, and wariness; people were unsure how to place us as a couple. I also encountered racism in Dubai when trying to get a job. In those days there were not many Indian women who had a professional job; they were mostly maids. When I applied for a job as a nurse, the head of nursing who was Lebanese, seemed taken aback that I was so confident, took a dislike to me, and refused to give me a work permit. This was so sad, as the head of the special baby care unit was desperate for English trained nurses. Instead, after yet another gruelling interview, I became a school nurse. The next step was employment in an English nursery; I was the first Indian to do this, but I'm happy to say I got the job based on my ability. The nursery head teacher afterwards told me that if I had had an accent, however, she would have never been able to employ me as the English parents would have objected.

I am proud to say that I am still breaking barriers and not being able to return to my nursing career steered me into the education world. Back in the UK, initially working in schools to support children, I was asked to set up the provision in one school for the children who have English as an additional language. I had never considered a specialism, but discovered a passion, which continues fifteen years on. I could relate to the families who were newly arrived, to the children who had no English, to teachers and schools who had to provide for them and the necessity of effective integration, and was therefore well placed to be the one who helped join the dots. I was proud to be the only undergraduate to be enrolled in and undertake a Masters course on Ethnic Minority Achievement Certificate and get the highest marks in my dissertation. The successful set up in that one school in Milton Keynes led me to be seconded out to the local authority to do some 'raising standards' work with a number of schools and eventually I was employed by the council to be an advisor to schools. Over the last ten years I have supported schools in raising their standards in the provision for black and minority ethnic pupils and have formed some very strong relationships with the schools. About two years ago, I decided to step even further out of my comfort zone and set up an independent consultancy company – doing what I do but within, and outside of Milton Keynes. It is hard work but so worth it to be in charge of my own destiny. Now, more than ever, I feel my work is needed to help people understand equality and being part of the global world, and if I can get one pupil/person to think about their thoughts, attitudes, actions, and have more empathy with others then I will be affecting change.

    My boys are now grown up and are independent and I could not be more proud of them. At times, I have felt really guilty, as much of their formative years, I had been struggling to adjust to a chronic illness. They have been forced to be self-sufficient. Living with inflammatory bowel disease has been and continues to be an uphill struggle. Juggling a full time job, children, husband running his own business, elderly parents who need more and more support adds to the stress of managing the condition. There have been some really low points and I have considered giving up my job many times. However, joining the local support group for National Association of Crohn's and Colitis and being on the organising committee has helped immensely. I now work with the organisation on a voluntary basis to help others and fund raise. The group has been my lifeline at times, as has been my husband and children who have infinite amount of patience and independence so I can continue to have a professional life as well some quality to my personal life.

I have also recently become involved in supporting the Syrian refugee families through my work with the Milton Keynes Middle East Cultural Group and Language School. I can empathise with these families to a certain extent and hope to make a difference. Their experiences are so profoundly heart breaking and I hope that my experiences personally and professionally will go some way to supporting the families to settle in safely and happily.

All the challenges in my life, the move to the UK, achieving in schools, nursing, finding my place in the education field, inter-racial marriage, raising two children with dual heritage, constantly moving and relocating and being diagnosed and living with a chronic illness has made me a stronger person. My life experiences so far have exposed me to some amazingly brave and inspirational people and opened my mind to our similarities and differences. I have made some fantastic friends along the way, many who have become friends for life as we have shared something rare. Life is never dull and I now strive to develop my work and with Simon by my side, create a sound and secure home for my family. I am so lucky to still have both my parents and am consciously making an effort to spend as much time with them as possible.

Despite all the struggles, I am forward thinking – I consider myself truly blessed.

Biography

A registered sick children's nurse and general nurse, Sejal worked at Great Ormond Street Hospital and Southampton General Hospital before marrying and moving to the Middle East with her husband. After eleven years abroad, living in Dubai, Muscat, Nairobi and Mombasa, she and her family returned to the United Kingdom. Here she diversified into education, specialising in raising the achievement of ethnic minority pupils. She strives to fight gender and racial inequality through education and is passionate about promoting the welling being of children. She has very strong relationships with her schools and is greatly respected and valued in her field of expertise. A few years ago, she took the brave step to become a freelance Education Consultant and is now developing this business.

In her spare time, being a sufferer, she volunteers to raise awareness of the life changing condition of Crohn's disease and Colitis, and is a governor for a small but very diverse nursery school. She loves to cook, is a member of a book club and enjoys travelling with her husband and family.

www.sejalpayneeducation.com

www.crohnsandcolitis.org.uk

Chris Ramsbottom

Sometimes a prescribed medication can have the adverse effect and even kill you, Chris is lucky to be alive. As is typical of all Women of Spirit, Chris turned her experience into a positive by opening her own holistic therapy centre in Coventry. She literally dreamed about her centre, convinced that this is what she is meant to be doing with her life, and that her success is a form of 'payback' for being allowed to live.

I FOUND MYSELF ON THE FLOOR in the flour aisle in Morrison's. How did I get there? No idea. It was 8.30am on a Monday morning and the place wasn't exactly stacked out with people. I have no idea how long I was there either. So, I thought I'd better get up, get the stuff paid for, and go back home. I gulped the air down as best I could, headed for the checkout, paid up, got in the car, and drove home – then I called the doctor. It was, after all, the fourth time I'd found myself on the floor in a supermarket in four weeks.

When I eventually made it to the doctor, she listened to my story and said, "I think you've been having silent heart attacks".

My reply was "I think it's the blood pressure tablets you've given me!"

But she insisted I keep taking them, and completed the referral form for the cardiologist.

Over the next few weeks, I had a whole array of tests, all of which came back 'normal'. But boy did I feel anything but normal! I would sit for hours gasping for breath. When I did get up and walk, I could go maybe three or four steps before stopping and holding on to something. I generally felt lousy. Stairs were a nightmare and I was really glad I didn't have to go up them more than once a day. I didn't really work at the time: I was and, still am, a holistic therapist and I saw the odd client every so often, and I'd had to change the way I worked as a Reiki healer so I sat down for most of the time.

The appointment for the cardiologist arrived for 15th August 2012. This was two days after my husband had come back from our usual volunteering holiday: a fortnight's 'retox' working at the Great British Beer Festival in Olympia. I hadn't gone this time, missing only the second year since 1981. Hubby had only worked during the set-up and take-down periods this year, coming home to keep his eye on me during the opening sessions, so he'd missed the festival completely!

The London Olympics were taking place at this time. As I love watching sport I looked forward to viewing the Games on TV. However I soon found that when excited I became breathless; the world would turn grey and spin quickly. Even during 'Super Saturday' all I allowed myself was a quick YES!, a punch of the air and a change of Facebook status.

I turned up at the hospital at the allotted time. My husband wasn't with me. His excuse? Well after all, he did work at the hospital and really didn't want to turn up during his holiday – he might get asked to work! That was fine by me. When I got to the desk, the receptionist looked at me and asked me not to take a seat, but to come through with her. I sat on a large seat and had measurements taken, including my blood pressure. And again, my blood pressure, a few minutes later, another blood pressure measurement. Then into a side room and another. Half an hour later, another one. What was going on?

Another half hour wait, and the doctor told me I was seriously ill and he wanted me to be admitted as soon as there was a bed available on the ward.

"You can't do that!" I said. "I have a client booked in for tonight!"

He did the old doctor thing of looking down his nose at me and said, "If you don't come in now you won't be seeing clients for some time!"

I managed to negotiate that I could return home and get an overnight bag and my husband and come back – which I did.

The day after, the head cardiologist came to me and sat on the bed and asked me why I was taking this particular blood pressure tablet, to which I replied that the doctor had said that I would be on it for life. His words didn't really sink in for quite a while afterwards: "Well I'm telling you that if you don't stop taking them, you'll be dead within three weeks!"

The discharge note said it was a 'bradykinin' response. Apparently, the drugs I'd been given for my high blood pressure were causing the natural hormone bradykinin to remain and not get broken down, which was causing in this instance, swelling of the mucous membranes in my lungs. This meant they didn't actually work properly, and by the time I'd got to hospital, my lungs were reduced to functioning at only about ten percent. This is not a rare side effect but it's not common either, and I was to only take the tablets prescribed by the hospital, which I began to do. It had taken me thirteen months to get to the near-death state I was in on the 15th August, and it would take me another thirteen months at least to get to anything approaching full health.

Fast-forward to 29th December 2014, and I am sitting in a room in an office block in Birmingham, waiting for a class to start. The course tutor said to me: "So Chris, what goals have you set yourself for 2015?"

I replied, "Oh I don't really do goals Dave. I have rheumatoid arthritis and every time I set a goal, my body conspires against me and I don't achieve it, so I don't bother. I do a good line in 'what if?' though."

It was what Dave said next that worked the magic. They do say that the question makes all the difference, and so it proved in this instance. "What would you say, if I told you that whatever you said, would succeed?"

My response came from a completely different planet to the one I had inhabited for the past ten years or so. "Oh, I'd have my own holistic therapy centre." The next thing I said was "Where the hell did that come from?"

It was certainly not on my radar, not on my wish list, not on my to-do list.

It was not what I wanted to do with my life. Not at that point, anyway.

Three days later I'm outside the bank, on Ball Hill in Coventry, having deposited a cheque. I parked my car on one of the side streets opposite and was waiting to cross the road using the pedestrian crossing. While waiting to cross I looked upwards and to the left instead of across to the right where the car was parked. "Oh, that's interesting" I thought, as I looked at the building with the 'To Let' sign on the first floor. 'I'll google it when I get home'. Which is what I did, and I found that the estate agents had put internal photos on their website. "Well it's a bit big for little old me, but I'll put in an enquiry and see what happens" I thought.

The day after I had a phone call from someone who told me he was the landlord of the property and asked what was I wanting to do with it. I told him I wanted to make it into a Holistic Therapy Centre and he said, "Well so do I". At this point my jaw bounced off the floor! "But I'm a builder, and I just want to deal with someone who wants to run it."

So, we arranged to meet, and obviously he could see some sort of potential in me because we met again and he started to do the building works needed to bring it up to modern standards.

Where on earth was I going to find the money to do this?

I applied for a Start-up Loan, and they took eight weeks to tell me that what I was proposing was too close to my field of expertise and they wouldn't fund it! Next port of call: the local community reinvestment trust, who were very interested and thought it was a great project, but they were too nervous of the market to give me any money. The darkest point came when my husband refused to extend the mortgage for me and then

I had to seriously consider what I was doing.

Over this period, I had become convinced that this was indeed what I was meant to be doing with my life, a form of 'payback' for being allowed to live in 2012. I had dreamed in the past of this – literally, I had had dreams about the stairs up to the Centre, and I was now having dreams about what the Centre would look like and what form it would take. I would wake up at 3am with pictures in my mind, procedures in place, and I'd write them down with the pen and pad I kept beside the bed – but in the morning, I couldn't actually read it because it had been dark when I wrote it and I wasn't wearing my glasses! So, I created a Facebook page, did an Indiegogo crowdfunder to raise some money which paid for my website to be created, and started to build a community of people who would support me. The Chamber of Commerce provided me with twelve hours of free business advice, and by a stroke of luck the advisor was someone I'd worked alongside in a previous job!

One morning I was half-awake listening to the radio and I heard a headline that many fifty-six-year-old women were taking their pension pots out and using the lump sum to fund various ventures. I thought "Well I'm fifty-six. I wonder if I can do this?" So, I did some research and worked out that I did indeed have some small pension pots. One I couldn't touch as it was a local authority superannuation fund, but two of them I could take out. If I let them mature, I would get maybe enough money each month to buy a bag of groceries. But if I took them out, I could finance my business with them and have enough money for some working capital while it established too! So, I thanked my nineteen-year-old self who took out a pension with the Prudential all those years ago, and scrimped and saved to pay the contributions, and got the process underway.

Now let me tell you about Saint Expedite. I didn't know about him but one day his details were shared to my Facebook page. He was a Roman soldier, who had the amazing ability to bilocate (be in two places at once) and who specialised in turning up with the resources just in time. He usually carried a staff with the legend 'Hodie' on it (which translates as 'Today'), and I must admit to praying to him at this stage. And yes: the money arrived two days before I was due to pick the keys up! I now have a little shrine to him at the Centre, where he is represented by a wooden Roman soldier doll I found online. He's never let me down!

And so here I sit at the Amethyst Centre a year and a couple of months later. We are still here and that is a joy and a blessing. I have plans to create a string of Amethyst Centres across the Midlands because I am quite sure that, as the NHS is run down and people find themselves thrown on to their own resources to manage their health, they will need to access the facilities such centres can offer. We offer a place where people can access therapies that aren't available on the NHS and some that are too. We also have a space where people can have meetings, run training courses or come and bring their laptop and access our free wi-fi and work. The Centre is an amazing oasis of calm on a busy main road in Coventry, with amazing vibes and we have a lot of therapists who want to work from here.

What makes me so determined? I need to tell you that I am an Aries and that makes me very awkward, determined to have my own way, and if I can't have my own way I would literally rather give up or die! The quickest way to get me to do something is to tell me either it can't be done, or that under no circumstances am I to even attempt to do it. My husband knows this, and I think it's behind his refusal to extend the mortgage so I could fund my dream. It didn't make for a very happy married life at the time though.

While I was growing up, my mother was a devoutly religious Christian, having been converted at a Billy Graham rally in the 1950s. My father was an equally devout atheist, having lost his faith in the jungles of Burma during World War II. This made growing up as someone with spiritual abilities distinctly challenging and 'character-forming'!

During the time between the "Shit, where did that come from?" moment and actually getting the Centre running, I had a series of psychic readings and also dreams which told me that if I did this, the spirit world would be right behind me, ensuring that it would succeed and all I had to do was go with the process. This is what made me determined to carry on, because it became clear that this project was indeed 'payback' for being allowed to live in 2012, it was my life's purpose and I had to trust the process. So, this is what I ended up doing, and it's what keeps me going now.

Biography

Chris was born in Birmingham, the only child of a foundry worker and a secretary. She was the first child in her family to go to university. She knew she had a gift for healing when, as an eight-year-old girl, she placed her hands on her mother's ailing washing machine and it sprang into life! After witnessing a miracle, where an old lady's swollen hand was returned to normal when Chris prayed over it when she was seventeen she decided that all this healing stuff was too scary and so she decided to run away from it. She did know she wanted to work with people, however, and did a social studies degree at Wolverhampton Polytechnic. During this time, she met and married her first husband. She trained as a counsellor but didn't complete the case study hours because she was given bereaved parents to counsel – not a good thing when you're twenty-two and having your own miscarriages! She left her first husband and moved to Yorkshire, married a Yorkshireman, and worked in further and higher education for some years.

Some years later, quite by chance, she encountered an amazing lady who encouraged her to go back to her spiritual healing abilities and develop them. She moved to Coventry, where she became a Teaching Reiki Master and trained in Complementary Therapies and set up her own practice in Warwick. However, this folded because her landlady didn't pay her landlord and he wanted the therapists to leave! She tried to continue her practice, and rented rooms where she could – which takes us to the start of this story. She is so grateful for the second chance at life that she has been given.

She is married to Steve and has three cats. Her ambition is to retire to the country and grow things.

www.amethystcentre.com

Jo Parfitt

As an expat expert, Jo has combined her passion for words with her experiences of living abroad to create a perfect portable career. Living in different and diverse countries for the past twenty years has created challenges for Jo, both as a wife and mother, and as a career woman driven to succeed wherever life and her husband's career took her. Flexibility and being a natural networker have been important ingredients in Jo's success as a writer, journalist, speaker, teacher, and publishing consultant.

IF I DO HAVE A TALENT then my talent is for writing. Words have always been my passion.

I was twenty-one when I met Ian. He was in England when we got together, but six months later was posted to Dubai, and for two years we conducted our relationship at a great distance. After we married, we lived in Dubai for six years, but I was homesick for the whole time. Despite this I was able to learn to be a journalist, which I absolutely loved. For me, work overseas meant that people wanted to know about me and I liked that. I do like people to recognise my name in a local paper! I loved Dubai for all the learning, I had my children there, and it was a great lifestyle. Our next posting was to Oman and there I was happier than I'd been anywhere in my life because we had the best friends, the weather was wonderful, Ian was happy, and I was doing journalism and writing books. I like being a features journalist, because I'm more interested in what makes people tick. I like to paint a picture – it's the storyteller in me. Next, we went to Norway, and there was no work for me, which made me so unhappy. Everything froze. Living there was prohibitively expensive, and it rained every single day for eighteen months. We both decided we would leave expat life and come back to England, and while the boys and I lived in our cottage in Rutland, Ian commuted to Gatwick for a year.

We lived in England for seven years, and for six of them Ian worked away from home during the week. He wanted the boys and me to join him, but I wouldn't. I've really regretted this, but I just wasn't ready. This was a massive risk, and it took Ian years to forgive me, but we are stronger than ever now.

I've been a freelance writer, author, teacher, and mentor for more than thirty years, which suits me – I've become such a free spirit. Writing has always been my outlet, my way of processing everything that's going on in my head: through writing a diary, speedwriting, poetry and by using writing as a career – which provided an income, that in turn validated me. I used to judge myself on my earning power. I was completely driven because it was the only place I could see my identity. Deep down I think I have low self-esteem. I don't know why, probably the main reason was that at university it always seemed that all my friends had a boyfriend and not me, and this gave me a 'nobody loves me' complex. I know that I felt that if somebody married me, then I must be loveable. And so, for me, the moment I got married I was able to be myself. It was my fundamental first step: get married and then be someone. The most important thing in my life has always been my marriage and my family, but a very close second has been my career. I would never sacrifice my family for my career, but I would sacrifice almost anything else.

I have now found myself, most definitely, but it took me until I was forty to start working on myself, to start really questioning why I was so obsessed with work. I used to say, when I was giving lectures, that I only had a professional and not a personal identity. It wasn't until I turned forty that I began to believe I might be of personal value to people; my career began to be less important though I had inadvertently become a workaholic. It was not until I had a burnout at fifty-one that I learned my lesson and began to have some balance in my life. Work is still an intrinsic part of me, but friends are more important and I now realise I am of value.

I have learned so much about working overseas and about how to be a writer and make money at it, writing about what I know. Going on stage to share my expertise and watch light bulbs switch on in everybody's heads, and have people coming up to me to say, "thank you so much" and "you changed my life," is hugely rewarding. This happens frequently, so now I have no fears going on stage. To begin with I was so terrified that my knee-caps would jiggle up and down and I'd get a dry mouth. Practise, in the end, made perfect, and I am a firm believer that we need the fear in order to create the adrenalin we need to perform at our best. I worry if I am not nervous. I want to share what I've learned to help others grow.

After our stint in England we moved to Holland for almost ten years. Holland was amazing. I wanted to go, I was fed up with being away from Ian and I wanted us to be a family again. But leaving my support network was tough. I recognised that I was a bit depressed for the first year. But Holland is a spiritual place, we all cycle and the landscape and art fed my soul. I built my business there and began helping people to write and publish their books in addition to the journalism and teaching. In 2013, we moved to Kuala Lumpur and we would have liked to stay abroad until Ian retired but that is now unlikely because of the demise of the oil industry. Our posting was cut short and we are now back in Holland. After the disappointment of our UK repatriation I had low expectations of this move but have been happily surprised. I love it here. It's familiar. I have a ready-made support network and many friends are married to locals so it is not a transient community. Travelling becomes much harder as the children (and our own parents) grow. Our children felt very un-rooted while we were away. Malaysia was our first 'empty nest posting' and it was tricky. Used to filling my days with work but post burnout I realised I could no longer hole myself up in my office. It was lonely at times but my work-life balance was never so good. Though our children are now in their twenties and highly mobile themselves they express a deep need for us to stop moving. I feel I have come through a difficult transition, but am now the person I was always meant to be, who is, quite simply, a writer.

I have long held a dream of running writing retreats, a place where people like me get to be together in a safe space and be inspired to write. I used to believe this could only be achieved once we stopped moving and bought a large house from which to run them. Now I know that there is another way to achieve this and I can rent cottages and hotel rooms in different countries and travel, teach, and inspire all at the same time. In 2017 the 'Writing Me-Treat' was born and takes place in Malaysia, England, Holland, France, and Italy to start with. No longer can I put my life and my dreams on hold.

For me, the toughest thing to cope with has always been the exhaustion of endings and beginnings. The packing up of face-to-face friendships, homes and businesses is bad enough but when you start again in a new place you have to start from scratch. I tend to leave one place being a big fish in a small pond who enjoys being known in the community and then arrive in another completely unknown again. With a business that survives by networking and word of mouth marketing it can be a real drag starting over again and again. The thing is it always takes about two years to get a business really going and when you have shortish postings this means that it feels as if I've just got going when it has been time to leave again. This has been the hardest of all. Moving the home and the family is a cinch compared to this! However, I could not be totally happy without work and as I love what I do so much, I always find the motivation in me somewhere to keep on reinventing myself and move on. Although the Internet and access to email have made it less difficult to network in a new community, it doesn't really get easier the more you do it. Over time, it wears you down. However, I am a firm believer that where there are endings there are beginnings and that challenges are just opportunities in disguise. Without constant upheaval, I'd soon be bored. All in all, I think I am probably hooked on it, however difficult it may be!

Biography

Jo Parfitt is a writer, editor, author, publisher, author's mentor, speaker, teacher, and serial expatriate who has managed to maintain and grow a portable business despite thirty years on the move. She is happily married to a chap who works in oil and has two grown sons who inevitably do not live in the same country as she does.

www.summertimepublishing.com
www.expatbookshop.com
www.joparfitt.com
www.writingmetreats.com

Helen Dickson

An emotionally neglectful childhood, constant diplomatic postings for her father and her parents' subsequent bitter divorce left Helen in fear – fear of being alone, fear of not sleeping, of being the only person awake in the house, and the belief that she didn't truly exist. Marriage to a charming man who turned out to be controlling and violent was as damaging, until, for the sake of her twins, she found the strength to leave.

MY EARLIEST MEMORIES ARE FROM ABOUT four years old. I have very happy memories of being in India with my brother who is two years older, we were great pals and I can remember so much about all the different things we used to do together. I recall going to school in the morning and swimming in the pool in the afternoons, we loved to play for hours in the gardens.

Memories of my father are vague. He worked in the diplomatic service and was always around in the background. He was there, but emotionally absent. He drank Heineken beer and listened to the BBC World Service. We had lots of servants. I shared a room with my sister and her ayah (nanny) but I never really felt that I had anything to do with her. They seemed to be a unit together. My brother was the key figure in my life. The diplomatic life was demanding and my mother didn't like the coffee mornings or the 'ladies who lunch' or the 'one-up-manship'. She was very unhappy. I don't remember very much about my parents or spending enjoyable times with them at all. We had a Siamese cat, as my father always had a cat wherever he lived. I loved these cats.

We then went to Colombia when I was around eight years old. My father was moved to a new post every three years and this was when my brother was sent to a Catholic boarding school. I think we were only there for about nine months and that's when my parents split up. My memories of being there were awful. I desperately missed my brother. I must have subconsciously absorbed a lot of emotional upset from Mum and Dad. I only remember my father getting angry with me once. Apparently, I used to panic when I knew that they were going out, and because of diplomatic life that was most evenings. There were times when my mother had to come out of big important dinner parties to come home for me. People were concerned that I hadn't attended school for months, and apparently kept telling my mum to take me to a child psychologist because of my anxiety. I instinctively knew something was wrong with my parents' marriage; I remember them sitting at the dining table and my mother crying silently. I would watch her from the other room. There were no audible disagreements, yet I lived in a constant state of panic, and didn't understand why.

Although my mother was a cuddly mother, my childhood felt like an emotional void. I felt no sense of safety or warmth, and it left me with an overwhelming emptiness. I always felt absolutely alone.

My mother was very bitter about the divorce. She had no money. Whenever the post arrived in the morning, I can see her now sitting on the stairs; I had to get her a gin and a cigarette before she could even open any post from my father. This affected me deeply because it happened in the formative years when as a child I was of course developing my emotions. So, I went from that situation to endless tears at boarding school when I was sent at the age of nine; fortunately, I was only there for three years, but I hated every minute. The fear of being alone, fear of not sleeping, fear of going to bed at night, of being the only person in the house left awake while everyone else slept only increased my unhappiness and anxiety.

My brother had ultimately disappeared, swallowed up with his own issues, and my father had abandoned me. My mother always used to leave a light on upstairs; I would doze and then wake up and have to go to the door to see if the light was still on. If the light had gone out I would start to panic; but then if I could see the light under her bedroom door I got a feeling of overwhelming relief that I was not alone in the world. I would have to go back for another look over and over again until eventually her light had gone. Then the panic started. I remember I had a pyjama case dog called 'Snowy'. I used to lie really straight in bed with the dog by my side and believed that if I didn't move I'd be safe.

Sometimes, I still feel that fear. Night time can be difficult. However, a therapy called EMDR (Eye Movement Desensitisation and Reprocessing) has been absolutely, incredibly brilliant for me. It made me realise the high level of tension I was holding in my body, and just how many individual issues were causing me pain – both emotional and physical. I now sleep so much better, and most of my nightmares have gone.

I lived with the belief that I was not important, that I didn't truly exist, that I was invisible. I was driven to do my very best with everything I did because then someone might notice me. This need to do things well is still excessive at times. Part of this deep-seated aloneness made me highly organised and I only felt safe if I was prepared for everything. I had no belief or expectation that anybody would help or do something for me, and I found it hard to ask anybody for any help. I had to do it all myself. I yearned to have somebody who I could really trust to look after me and care for me. I met my first boyfriend at sixteen. It was very innocent, he would walk me home after school and my mother used to charge him for coffee! My mother criticised every boyfriend I had and left me with little self-confidence or self-esteem; I couldn't understand why anyone would want to go out with me.

I really wanted to work with animals, to be a vet, but my disrupted schooling meant that my grades let me down. My mother suggested that I became a nurse. So, I did. I applied to six nursing schools and was accepted by all of them. I was too petrified to enjoy such a positive outcome and chose to study to become a Registered General Nurse at Manchester Royal Infirmary over Oxford because, ironically, I was terrified of leaving my mother.

The need to be totally self-sufficient became more marked when I was with my first husband. It was the Edinburgh Festival and I was around twenty- five years old. One evening my friend and I couldn't decide if we should go out or not, and as we couldn't be bothered to get dressed up, we went round to the local pub and bumped into Jack. He was absolutely charming; I remember feeling very comfortable with him. I don't know why. I realised later he was quite a cold detached person, and in that way reminded me of my father – maybe that's where the familiarity came from. For a while he made me feel safe. He was big, well-built, tall, dark and in control – very in control of himself and his life, and that probably alleviated my anxiety, making me feel safe. I felt a great sense of belonging to somebody. All of a sudden, I was important. Somebody wanted me. We had a simple home-made wedding and honeymooned in Cyprus.

I cried throughout my entire honeymoon. It was the most miserable, unhappy time of my life. Jack was so aggressive and every evening as he drank more and more, he would become progressively more nasty until he made me cry. I felt worthless. As soon as the ring was on my finger, the 'real' Jack emerged. If I said the 'wrong thing' the atmosphere would change and an awful argument would ensue, ending with me in tears, every single night. He was rough and horrible to me even in bed. How could I have missed the signs? Why did I go into marriage so quickly? I was certain that there was absolutely nothing before we were married that could ever have made me expect such a change of character.

I had to move down to London to join Jack. Moving was very hard;

I had two cats, it was the first time I had been able to choose to have two cats and not to have to fight for the right to have them. My mother wanted me to get rid of the cats, Jack wanted me to get rid of the cats, but I was damned if I was going to, so the cats came too. Those two cats were gentle and affectionate but Jack was very cruel to them which upset me; I used to try and keep them out of his way.

I was living in a nightmare. I was alone and couldn't tell anyone what was happening to me. It didn't feel real and I just hoped it would settle. Jack was already beginning to get angry at the slightest thing and this frightened me.

Then my Dad became very ill and died within a week. It was a very sudden tragic event which has haunted me ever since. In life he had been an absent father and we never made the opportunity to resolve this, and now he was gone forever. Jack actually took care of me and was very supportive, but it was his birthday the day after my father died, and he was angry because I had nothing arranged for his birthday. His anger horrified me, I couldn't comprehend why a person could react like that. I panicked thinking I had done something wrong. Instead of standing up for myself as my father had just died in horrific circumstances, I blamed myself for being a failure of a wife.

I remember him describing himself as 'a knight in shining armour'. He always talked about loyalty and integrity, but our marriage was in serious trouble; we were in separate bedrooms and ultimately only remained in the same house for financial reasons. He started seeing different girls while he was still living with me, and would come to me, yes me, to ask advice about how he should progress in the relationships. At his lowest times he told me that he believed he was a narcissist, and described himself as being on a totally different plane to everybody else. He would launch straight into deep conversations and was a great performer. I was still vulnerable – he made me laugh and that's a very powerful thing; if somebody makes you laugh, that can be incredibly attractive. It was Jack's intelligence and articulate conversation that impressed me and it felt comfortable and familiar – my father was very intelligent and had studied at Cambridge.

There were other clues to Jack's controlling nature that I missed. He was not happy when I became pregnant. He started to get violent and was frequently aggressive and angry. I cried just about every day of my pregnancy and wondered whether antenatal depression would automatically lead on to post-natal depression?

The twins were six weeks premature and tiny; I was in hospital for three weeks, and was up all day and night giving them hourly feeds. The day after they were born Jack made me stand on the weighing scales in the ward. I had lost weight after my father's sudden death and had been eight stone before I discovered I was pregnant. After delivery I weighed nine and a half stone. He then told me how much I would need to lose. At first, Jack tried very hard to help with the twins but he just couldn't do it without getting highly frustrated. I went back to work just before they were six months old and Jack did some of the childcare around his shifts as well as hiring a part-time child-minder. He used to laugh because the twins were both frequently very sick and we had to deal with projectile vomiting daily, which went on for months. His laughter scared me, his behaviour and reactions just didn't feel right for a parent. I am convinced that the twins' sickness was because the two of us were so stressed and the whole atmosphere was so tense.

Then I discovered he had started to try and upset all my efforts caring for the babies. He would deliberately dirty a sterilised spoon or bottle teat before using it, as if he was jealous of the attention I paid to caring for the babies. I functioned like a robot, everything was immaculately organised. I remember going to the hospital at three months and the doctor telling me that my babies were doing superbly well; they looked so well dressed and so well cared for. He asked how I was, but I couldn't answer as I struggled to hold back the tears. I used to dread leaving the twins with Jack. When they were crawling, and were ready for a sleep he would never put them into bed. They would just crawl around the floor until they finally collapsed and went to sleep where they fell. He used to leave pins on the coffee table when they started to get to the toddler stage, just to leave dangerous things in their way. The first time he looked after them for a whole day, came the first violent episode. As I came in from work, he turned around and said, "Make me a cup of tea." And I replied, "I'm just in the door!"

His foot came at me and smashed me in the face. I had been at work all day – I knew I didn't deserve it but thought I must have been a bad wife. Eventually I got to the point where I could see it coming, but couldn't stop it happening. My confidence and capability was so eroded, I simply couldn't leave.

We went round and round in circles and it was just awful. I finally managed to persuade him to go, but soon after he arranged to meet me one day, told me he was missing our routine and the children, so he was coming back. I suffered panic attacks for weeks but I couldn't do anything about the situation. I had got so used to it, I just got my head down and got on with it, and we ended up buying a bigger house. I thought it would be fine, things would be better, but we still went round in circles. He used to drink and drink, and I found myself trying to drink at least as much as him to get more out of the bottle so he would drink less. I was prepared to do anything to gain more control. I was not prepared to accept the violence anymore, and was ferociously protective of my children.

I looked after the twins, household chores, the garden, home maintenance, car, decorating, birthdays, Christmas – everything. I went over and over in my mind how I could manage without him and wrote down how much everything would cost – and could never make it balance. I dealt with all the bills anyway. For the last two years he was with us the twins and I spent Christmas in Manchester and I stopped adding his name to the Christmas cards. We just ignored him as much as we could apart from when he got angry – and then it felt like the whole world was crashing down on my head. I was so determined to protect my children and stop him from harming their futures, so I had a free consultation with a lawyer and wasn't even sure what I needed to ask. I showed him all my monthly household figures and how hard it would be, and I asked if he thought I would manage. I remember he said: "You're not very vindictive, are you?"

All I could think of was that we would manage somehow and would be better off without Jack. I pictured myself as a lemming jumping off a cliff without having a clue what would happen.

Jack still wouldn't go but I managed to get him out of the bedroom into the spare room where he was for a further six months. The stress was horrendous and my shoulders were permanently stiff and hunched. I had to listen to all his woes about this and that girlfriend, how to manage his new relationships, sit in one room as he spent hours on the phone in the other room to one or other girl.

Finally, he announced that he had bought a flat and was moving out. No warning, no thought about the existing financial commitments he had – the house and four-year-old twins. He forced me to sell the car and demanded that I gave him have the money, and then he went. He didn't give me any maintenance for the first two years and after that only when forced by the child support agency, who eventually had to arrest his wages. The day he left I stopped taking sleeping tablets. I was thin and exhausted but determined.

I had a full-time nursing job and I also worked every Saturday night in a nursing home to help pay the bills. The long-term stress and working such long hours caused chronic back pain. A twelve-week programme called DBC Active Spine Care taught me how to manage the pain, continue to function, and to understand the psychological relationship between physical and psychological pain. I had au pairs because that was the only way I could afford child care. I would come out of the nursing home absolutely shattered and walk wearily down the road, passing a local paper shop. One day the owner Michael offered me a lift home. Then he started dropping the papers off at the nursing home just as I came out. Eventually he told me to use his car. He was so unassuming, and so patient with me. He was so good with the kids and they had fun together, but it was months before I could let him stay. He had a trouser press the same as Jack's and just the ticking noise made me go cold inside. I knew I had to face my fears, the poor man couldn't live the rest of his life not putting his trousers in a trouser press!

I learned to trust in Michael, and in myself, and we married when the twins were eleven years old. A few months into being married, we had the house all done up, and I was happy for the first time in my life. I felt comfortable, I felt safe, I had enough money to live on – and I sank into an incredible depression. I was terrified of losing it. I went to counselling because I realised I didn't understand what was happening to me – crying every morning was just weird. Cognitive behavioural therapy helped me understand how I 'ticked' – the efficiency, coping, determination, the nightmares about Jack and my father's death. I also needed to address Jack's violence and the fear which gripped me with things like Michael leaving a tie on the bannister, the sound of the trouser press timer, the total panic when we switched the light off at night. We tried moving the furniture in the bedroom to try and make different, but the terror never stopped until we built an extension and moved into a different bedroom. Counselling helped me understand my emotions and to trust in Michael and the happiness he provided. EMDR – eye movement desensitisation and reprocessing – was dramatic, definitely the most effective.

Now, I understand my fears and I self-protect a lot more. I've got a good job as a practice nurse and am fulfilled caring for others, I'm well respected and I have held it together. Our marriage is a fantastic partnership. We are finely tuned and understand each other. I've always been conscious of trying to do right by my children; listening to them, worrying about spoiling them, worrying about not giving them what they needed both materially and emotionally, trying to value them and respect them, and now they have grown into wonderful adults. When the four of us are together we have a great time with lots of laughter. We are a family.

In 2008 Michael and I wrote a huge business plan, took out a massive bank loan, created our dream home in the country, and built a state of the art cattery. This has satisfied my lifelong dream to work with animals. We are often fully booked, and have a fantastic reputation. I married my best friend who looks after me and makes me laugh every day; our children are strong and happy, live independently and love to come home. I value myself enough to get my nails done, indulge in beauty treatments, and I am, at last, happily surrounded by cats!

Biography

Helen trained as a registered general nurse at Manchester Royal Infirmary from 1981-1984 and subsequently lived in Edinburgh. She has worked for over twenty years as a practice nurse and is highly qualified and experienced in her field. Helen and her husband Michael built a brand-new cattery and have worked hard together to develop it into a highly successful business.

www.catseyecattery.co.uk
www.emdria.org
www.spirehealthcare.com
www.dbcactivespinecare.com
www.nct.org.uk/parenting/postnatal-depression

Three

Perfect in My Imperfections

I will either find a way, or make one.

Anon

Victoria Petkovic-Short

At twenty-one, the loss of her femininity and identity – in an age where we are bombarded by the media with 'flawless perfection' – was devastating to Victoria's emotional wellbeing. Choosing to take ownership, not to be defined by her condition, and in-spite of some harrowing times, she now campaigns to improve body-confidence and self-worth.

IF THERE IS ONE THING I have learned in the last five years, it is that we waste an inordinate amount of time fearing the inevitable or, worse yet, fearing the un-inevitable events that lie ahead. I was no different and as a twenty-one-year-old university graduate, I was equal parts excited and terrified by the future prospects I had.

For me, my life was not turned inside-out by applying for jobs or moving back in with my parents; it wasn't an adjustment back into family life or leaving behind my friends that left me bereft and in turmoil. For me it was a total and complete loss of my identity and femininity, an event entirely out of my control and uniquely devastating to my emotional wellbeing, yet one I had never even contemplated as a risk.

I remember standing on a garage forecourt in 2011, pumping petrol into my car on a blustery April morning. The wind whipped across the courtyard and while my attention was partially on the nozzle in my car, more prominently it was split between a car full of teenage boys on the next pump over, and the challenge of keeping my head still. At the time, I was inexplicably losing my hair, and only my very specifically-styled hairdo covered the tell-tale bald patch the size of a digestive biscuit. Until that morning, I had been rather blasé about my hair loss; I'd like to tell you I was handling it brilliantly, but in reality, I was in wholehearted denial – an option available to me because of the snail-paced progression of my hair loss and my intrinsic faith in a quick-fix cure. Alas, whether a joke of the gods or simply bad luck, it was not my day to escape unnoticed. The wind blew, whipping in eddies around the cars and the pumps and blowing my hair into a frenzy around my face. I turned, scrabbling frantically with one hand to pat down and re-cover my patches, but it was too late and I heard the guffaws before I turned red-faced to see the four teenage boys nudging each other and laughing at my expense.

Credit to myself, I summoned the will from somewhere, and left my hair blowing casually in the breeze, staring down the teenagers with an air of nonchalance, while inside I felt I would dissolve from the shame and humiliation. Meanwhile, my soul was crumbling from the sudden realisation that there was no cure and it wasn't getting better. That was the first day I properly cried. Alone in a car, heading back to my parents' house, my hands gripped the steering wheel until my knuckles were white, but still the tears came, dripping from my chin and staining my jeans a darker shade of indigo. I gulped down sobs, harshly told myself to get a grip, and drove like a granny all the way home.

I have a condition called Alopecia Universalis. It is an auto-immune condition whereby my immune system has become overactive and confused, attacking healthy cells, including my hair follicles and leaving me with no hair on my head or on my body. Think about that for a moment. No hair; no eyebrows, no eyelashes. Nothing to style, frame my face or to flutter at my unwitting husband. True, as I have been informed many times "it's only hair", but in modern society it is so much more than that; it is a part of our identity, integral to our femininity, and we are encouraged to pursue flowing, healthy locks as a definition of our value and 'worth.' Physically, the lack of hair is irrelevant to everything except appearance – I am a little colder perhaps and more things drop in my eyes, but I am largely unchanged. Emotionally, it is as far from 'only hair' as you can possibly imagine. Without it, I felt unattractive, un-loveable and lost – without identity, no longer feminine and certainly not valued.

The forecourt incident was the start of my journey to self-love, self-value and self-confidence like I have never experienced before, and one for which I will always, always be grateful, despite remaining totally bald. It is also linked to my simultaneous discovery of the failings of our society to teach people, and particularly women, self-confidence and self-worth at all ages.

Growing up as a child, I was lucky to have parents who instilled a sense of self-worth and confidence in me, and who always encouraged me to do my best. It is thanks to these attributes and the continued support of friends and family that I have reached a point of unprecedented happiness and confidence in myself. After the shock of the petrol station and much time spent struggling with what was happening, I reached a second pivotal moment when I looked remarkably like 'Gollum' from 'Lord of the Rings' – or at least my hair did. Up to this point I had been lovingly clinging to my remaining hair as it continued to fall out, and although I knew I was past the point of regrowth and being able to disguise it naturally, I still refused to take ownership of the problem. I will never forget sitting on the floor, with my mum on the sofa trying to tease out the knots in the final patch of extremely matted hair, when I felt a sense of extreme exasperation with myself. I realised I was allowing myself to be overwhelmed by an emotional attachment, letting it change and mold who I was, when in reality I should be changing and molding what it was. I grabbed a pair of scissors and demonically demanded that my mum cut off the remaining hair, watching while she struggled to suppress the look of extreme horror on her face wondering whether I was making the right choice and if she should really do it.

The important thing was that I was making a choice. I was choosing to take ownership and control; I was choosing how to let it affect me; and I was choosing my self-value and self-worth as I asserted that hair loss wouldn't define me. It was perhaps the most impactful moment of my life, a moment when I realised that it didn't matter what others thought or felt or opined; it mattered how I thought, felt and reacted.

Since that day, I have done everything in my power to be positive and proactive with my condition. It has been far from easy, but always reminding myself that I am alive, well and generally pretty fun to be around (in my opinion of course), this has been a really important part of my recovery. Initially, I started to look for the positives in having my condition; simply dubbed 'the silver-lining game.' I challenged myself to think of one reason each day for one hundred days as to why my hair loss was a good thing. Some were straightforward, such as the money I save on the hairdresser, on shampoo, and on 'accessories,' to the frankly bizarre such as not getting hair in my food or getting it stuck in the zip, but it was important and life-affirming. This process reminded me that it doesn't matter how dire the situation, it is your response which matters and you can put yourself back in charge of your own destiny. This for me was and is a defining mantra and is now aptly dubbed 'mindfulness' although it wasn't a fashionable, well-documented technique back then. Our grandparents referred to it as 'mind over matter.'

My thanks must also go to the community of fellow 'apatchy warriors' that has been established by national charity Alopecia UK. By comparison, with many charities, AUK is relatively small, but it packs a powerful punch when it comes to awareness and support, boasting ambassadors such as Olympic Cyclist Joanna Rowsell-Shand and composer and musician John Altman. One thing that was consistent with my own journey was a sense of isolation; Alopecia is often disguised or hidden by those who have it, and is neither life-threatening nor 'sexy' enough to regularly make mainstream news. Although I was coping fairly well with the support of my family and friends, nothing came close to the weekend I spent in Liverpool, taking part in a 'Flash Mob' with more than sixty fellow 'baldies.' It was empowering, uplifting and motivational and certainly indescribable in terms of the freedom gained from meeting others who live with it too. The event wasn't a total happy conclusion however, and for me served to reinforce my understanding that hair loss can be brutal and in many cases life-destroying. I met people whose partners had left them, children and adults who had been bullied mentally and/or physically, who had suicidal thoughts, a total lack of self-belief and who had put their lives on hold as they tried desperately to hold onto their identity. I will never judge or condemn this collective however they may feel; I too have had some harrowing times and they are in many ways a bi-product of society and the expectations that we set for others. I cannot however overlook how truly condemning these expectations are and how life-altering they can be for someone who is 'different' from the norm, willingly or otherwise. Thankfully, many of those that I met then have continued on a largely positive journey, just like my own, and Alopecia UK continues to do an admirable job supporting and caring for and driving awareness and research. These journeys, my own and others, are also my inspiration to continue fundraising and encouraging body confidence however and wherever I can, even on a small scale.

Having met my, now, husband not long after the start of my hair loss, I struggled with the potential pressure that hair loss could put on our relationship and the potential loss of support I anticipated should he get cold feet. Despite promising to stay 'just friends,' Tim's support, care and persistence paid off, leading to a very happy relationship and later marriage. I will forever be grateful of the lessons learned in my relationship with Tim, that there are good people in the world without judgement, that there is always someone who will love you for who you are and importantly, that I must and should love myself always.

Along the way I have grieved for my hair; I have been through denial, anger, upset, a heap of guilt for being so upset, despite it not actually affecting my health; self-loathing, envy, bargaining, and finally a level of acceptance. It hasn't actually been a 'process' either, with my emotions jumping back and forth between the stages and even now, five years on, there are days when I am still upset, angry or frustrated. However, fundamentally, Alopecia has been good for me, for my self-confidence, for my happiness and ultimately for my life. I was single when I first started losing my hair and am now happily married with a husband that loves my confidence. I have been on 'Good Morning Britain,' on live radio, been in 'Cosmopolitan' magazine and on a winning 'Eggheads' TV quiz team; developed, launched and sold a nude, bald fundraising calendar, and this year will be a bald extra in a Sci-Fi movie. For me, Alopecia represents a land of opportunity; the opportunity to experience new things and push myself out of my comfort zone; the opportunity to meet new people and make a whole pile of new friends; the opportunity to raise awareness and giving me a passion to fundraise; and importantly the opportunity to help and support others to reach their own point of acceptance. I can honestly and confidently say that looking back, Alopecia has drastically changed me, but it has changed me for the better and I have never been more positive, confident, self-assured or happy. You will regularly see me bald, or with an ever-changing hairstyle thanks to my gorgeous wig collection, and I consider myself an incredibly lucky person, in spite of it all.

I have reached a stage in my journey where I am truly happy in myself; probably happier and more confident even than when I had hair. Some of that is of course age and maturity, but some of that comes from being challenged by change and coming out the other side smiling. If you offered me my hair back tomorrow on a shiny silver platter, no strings attached, it is honestly something I would have to consider very carefully. For me, I predict it would be an even harder journey back into the world of hairy, having to adapt both to the physical changes and the psychological impact of again losing a part of my identity. I'm not sure I am ready for that transition in reverse and I can honestly say I'm happy as I am and I don't need my hair back any time soon.

My dream now is to help others, and as well as offering help and support on a one-on-one basis, with everything from wigs to body confidence, or frankly just a natural chat, I also spend a lot of my time campaigning to improve body-confidence and self-worth of young people. For this, I will always be grateful, and if I could pass on one piece of advice it is this: To love and value yourself before all others, because in doing so you will find unprecedented strength and intrinsic happiness.

Biography

Victoria is an outgoing and driven individual, known for her tenacity and passion. She is an Account Director for a PR and Marketing Agency, which she owns and manages with her mum. She is married to a loving husband, soppy owner of two big dogs and an avid crafter. Victoria is now a keen body confidence coach, charity fundraiser and awareness advocate; when she can, spending time devising unique and eye-catching initiatives and supporting the charity Alopecia UK.

To make a donation to the charity, please do so via their website:
www.alopecia.org.uk
or via my Women of Spirit JustGiving page
www.justgiving.com/fundraising/bald-victoria

Mary Lunnen

Happily married for more than forty years, Mary put her creative skills to good use making jewellery until the recession of the 1990s hit hard. A change of direction led her to study for an MA with the Open University. Cancer diagnosis and subsequent surgery left Mary feeling that although Western medicine had saved her life, she was simply a bed number instead of a human being. She found the process so life-changing that she trained to be a coach and set up her own life-coaching practice.

REFLECTING ON LIFE IS ALWAYS, FOR me a challenge: how much is true memory? How much is drawn from family stories? How much has been influenced by the lens of time? Maybe not distorted exactly, more embellished in some places and with pieces missing in others.

My parents were of the generation who lived through the Second World War. I cannot imagine what that can have been like for them. They both told us something about their lives: as a child I was often not very interested, how I wish now I had paid attention, and even more, that they were still here to ask. Any challenges I may have faced seem on a different scale, though nonetheless, real and powerful too.

My earliest memory is of the day my brother was brought home for the first time after his birth in hospital. I was two and a half years old. I clearly remember being allowed to hold him as we sat on the back seat of the car on the way home. The awe I felt of this tiny, new, human being was strong, as was my love for him and joy at his arrival. I was so small myself, and remember nothing else for a long while afterwards, but I think the trust my mother had in me, and her thoughtfulness too, to allow me that moment was why that memory is so strong.

Looking back at that little girl, who is still within me, I feel I need to tell her to keep that joy, that optimism, that love. And then, connecting with her, with me, I know that she did. Through all the challenges that awaited; all the years; all the shocks and illness; births and bereavements; weddings and funerals; laughter and tears – she is still smiling, still loving, still joyful.

A few years after that first memory, at about five, I was very ill with rheumatic fever. My older sister had it even more severely and spent some time in hospital, but I was treated at home. I remember my mother having to carry me downstairs to a 'day bed'. I remember the time our cat jumped in through the window and landed on me as I was eating a bowl of pudding – which went everywhere. I remember the doctor coming to give me injections with a big needle.

There is something else from that time, another memory, that I lost touch with for years. A connection with the spiritual world. I believe we are all born with that connection still strong, but many of us lose it, maybe for a few years, or many, or forever. For me, that link remained for a while. I am not sure when it began to weaken, I only know that I lost it.

Certainly, from early teenage times and into adulthood I was searching, looking for something outside myself to fill a gap, a void I felt within me.

A long time later a partial memory surfaced from that time of illness as a child, I remembered hearing a voice. I remembered it being reassuring when I was frightened in the dark, probably calling for my mother. She would come and sing me a favourite lullaby 'I had a little nut tree'. It wasn't until even later in my life that the words the voice spoke returned to me.

During those years, I grew up, was injured in a car accident while at school, went to university, and travelled the world. I continued to look for things I thought were missing from my life – and in those years, I often focused on the mirage of romantic love. I call it a mirage: it is inspiring and sparks great works of literature, art and music. It has taken me a long time to see that – for me – if I follow a mirage it continually disappears and recedes into the distance.

I know myself to be more than lucky, to be truly blessed to have met a man I have spent forty years with now. Through the ups and downs of life, through the difficult times when it was touch and go, we have stayed with our marriage, sparked ideas, anger, laughter, learned from each other. And now we are growing older together.

We married in 1977, and, wishing to stay in the place we both loved, but with few jobs available, I decided to start making and selling copper enamel jewellery, encouraged by my mother. She had always been an example to me of a strong and entrepreneurial spirit, always having ideas for small business projects she could run from home, using her skills in design, knitting, art and crafts to bring in extra money for our family.

I built my business up slowly, working in restaurants part-time, traveling to craft markets and shows in my ancient car. I loved the colour and quality of enamels – glowing glass in so many different shades – and the unpredictability of the process of firing. I especially loved the 'scrolling' process that produced abstract swirling patterns within which all sorts of pictures emerged, depending on who was looking.

The business became successful and as well as exhibiting at shows and markets myself, I began selling to shops and galleries around the UK, and a few overseas, until a global recession in the early 1990s hit my sales hard. At the same time, I also felt I needed a change and had developed a longing to return to study, to learning, to 'check that my brain still worked'. After a considerable amount of discussion and compromise, I chose a distance learning MA with the Open University, and settled into studying – and into searching for an employed position to give me the confidence that I could pay the course fees. By 1992 I found myself working in a job full time, studying late into the night and in the early morning and – despite my enjoyment of it all – struggling. There was so much change going on: I felt I was growing and learning; coping with a job where for the first time I was in a management position. I felt under a huge amount of stress, for which I tried to get help, from my employer, and my family doctor. Somewhat ironically it was on a visit to the surgery to ask for this help that my doctor told me my regular cervical smear test had shown a problem that needed investigation.

This was in 1994 and the outcome turned out to be a pivotal point in my life: a diagnosis of cervical cancer. It could have destroyed my marriage: I feel it probably saved it. It could have destroyed me: I came through it – partly due to luck and quick treatment – as a survivor, and spiritually stronger. Now, after many years of dealing with physical pain which was the main side effect of my surgery, I can see that this awful experience was truly a turning point in my life: a wake-up call for me.

Almost the first thing I did was to buy a journal and start writing – sharing all my thoughts and fears that I felt I couldn't 'burden' my family and friends with. I now know that it is a common experience for people with a cancer diagnosis to find themselves protecting those around them from the rawness of their feelings about what is happening, when really, they need support themselves. My husband is a practical man, an engineer who fixes things, replacing parts that don't work to get machinery going again. He couldn't do that for me, for my malfunctioning body, and I imagine that was hard for him. So, my journal became somewhere I could 'voice' my thoughts and fears, as well as record what was happening to me.

Many cancer patients say people treat them differently. I noticed this immediately. My mother lived close by and I didn't want to break the news in a telephone call – though I had to do this with my husband who was at work. I had already called him once: that day I was in bed resting after a reaction to the investigation and treatment I had received as an outpatient following the abnormal smear. The phone rang: it was my doctor's receptionist asking me to come in and see her. This never happened: I knew something was badly wrong.

So, I had driven myself there, and sat in the empty waiting room, where even though the morning's appointments had finished, the piped music was still playing. The jingle-jangle of a pop song feeling very out of place to my ears. Once I had received the diagnosis, and been told what would happen next, I asked if I could speak to another woman who had been through this. My doctor said no, there was no mechanism to do this at that time due to patient confidentiality. There are now many organisations such as Macmillan Cancer Support, and – specifically for cervical cancer patients and their families and friends – Jo's Trust, but there was very little in 1994, and little in the way of support here in Cornwall.

In between when I called my husband the second time, and when he arrived home, I called my employer and gave her the news. When we returned from my mother's house after an hour or so, there was a big bouquet of flowers on the doorstep. A beautiful thought from my colleagues, wanting to show their support – and also a taste of being treated as Mary the cancer patient, not just Mary.

The first stage of my treatment, some ten days later, was surgery. On the first night after my operation – a major procedure called a Wertheim's hysterectomy – I lay awake in bed in severe pain. Drowsing on and off with the pain-killers not really helping much, at one point I clearly heard my mother singing 'I had a little nut tree' to me. At that time, I hadn't thought of that song for many years. The next day she told me she hadn't been thinking of the tune either, but had been sending me what she always called 'healing thoughts' – and that was how I had received them. Such a magical connection with my mother, and a link back to my childhood.

Many years later, towards the end of her life, I was able to talk to my mother about her wishes for her funeral. As was typical of her she said she 'didn't want any fuss'. We talked about the little nut tree song and she decided she would like to have that played and sung. When it came to the time tracking down the words and music proved quite a challenge, but I did, and the process provided some smiles through my tears.

Part of my recovery from my surgery for cancer was taking back control from the 'medical machine', that had left me feeling I was on a conveyor belt – being treated as 'the cervical cancer in bed number eight' instead of as a whole human being, as me. Western medicine had saved my life. It wasn't so good at dealing with the pain, nor at helping me with the emotional and spiritual support I needed. The first thing I did was to pay for some acupuncture treatments – they may have helped with the pain, but not with any dramatic effect. What that process – and the attention of the skilled practitioner, the conversation and the touch – did do was open me up to spiritual healing.

After a while I felt I needed to do something about the lack (at that time anyway) of information for women and their families about how other people have come through cervical cancer. I started interviewing women and collecting their stories, which were eventually published, partly self-funded and helped by a small publisher, the Hypatia Trust. The title was inspired by something we all felt, we just had to carry on: *Flying in the Face of Fear*.

From there so many things developed: involvement with cancer charities where I both offered and received support; trying other complementary therapies, and becoming a Reiki healer myself.

Through all this time, I found one of my biggest challenges, in addition to the physical pain, was coping with the change in my own body. I didn't look any different, apart from a long scar that no one could see. However, I had lost the most integral part of being a woman: my womb. Fortunately, I had already chosen not to have children. But now the decision was out of my hands anyway: I underwent an instant menopause the instant my ovaries were removed. Later, this was made easier to cope with by hormone replacement therapy (HRT). There was also an inevitable impact on my relationship with my husband.

In time, I went back to work, changing jobs several times partly from choice and partly through three experiences of redundancy. During the first of these I again took control – the employee support package included counselling and some career guidance, but I had just heard about life coaching and chose to buy this support for myself. I found the process so life-changing that I trained to be a coach and set up my practice, 'Dare to Blossom', in 2003, running it alongside other work as a business trainer and advisor within two different organisations.

All the while I was learning and growing, reading books, being involved with coaching as a coachee and attending other people's workshops, and beginning to develop my own.

During this time, in a meditation, I remembered hearing the voice, the one that spoke to me as I lay awake in the night as a small girl. It was another period of years before the words the voice spoke came back to me. Writing this now, I am smiling at myself as the key process I have developed that helps my coaching clients and the people who attend my workshops is based around the idea of 'rediscovery'. Rediscovering my inner wisdom – which I now believe the voice represents, even though, then, and in my memory, it came as if from an external entity.

I supported my mother, especially when she had a severe stroke in 1999 and had to live the rest of her life in various nursing homes. It felt like a gift to me that I was able to spend time with her sorting through old photos and family treasures when we had to sell her home to pay the fees. I know she would have preferred to have ended her life with that stroke, and, whilst understanding that, I often told her how grateful I was that, somehow, she had chosen to stay on. I was with her when she did pass away, a sad goodbye, and also a merciful release for her from pain and disability.

Since June 2015 I now find myself running my business full time – as a life coach, writer, artist – and a connector of people with others, and with themselves. When I was working and keeping 'Dare to Blossom' ticking over too, I weathered many ups and downs, hard knocks and celebrations. I learned so much about myself and shared knowledge and insights with others. It was in 2011, when planning a series of 'Dare to Blossom' workshops that the idea of the words on cards, each with a colour, came to me. Some of my first thoughts were along the lines of "who am I to think I can create anything new?" I loved my packs of angel cards and oracle cards.

Despite my doubts, I continued, buoyed by the awareness of how important words and colour have been to me throughout my life; confident that others would connect with them too. I created a pack of fifty cards, which I called the 'Dare to Blossom Rediscovery Cards'. After a while people began asking to buy them and the stories they told me of all the different creative ways they used them inspired me to continue. Now it feels as if I simply caught the idea out of the air as it was passing (as Elizabeth Gilbert has described in her 2015 book Big Magic) at the right time, and it has taken off into the world again.

The cards have developed a life of their own somehow: for me, and for others, often as a daily practice. I find just about everyone enjoys the chance to draw a card for themselves, and to reflect on the word and the colour. I use them as a conversation-starter when I am exhibiting at business shows and talking at events: offering someone a 'word for the day' and asking them what the word and the colour evoke for them prompts a conversation of a totally different quality and character than simply asking "What do you do?"

Sometime during the last few years, again during a meditation, I remembered the words spoken by the voice I heard when I was around five years old. The words?

"You are safe my child."

My own inner wisdom knew that then, in the dark night when I felt alone, frightened and in pain. And I know it still, in truth we are all safe, our inner light is eternal and cannot be extinguished. This keeps me motivated and moving forward in what is very much like starting up a new business at the age of sixty-four, still learning, still developing, still rediscovering and beginning, at last, to find, and release my power within.

Biography

Mary's first experience of mentoring was in the early 1990s as a volunteer with the Prince's Trust. Since that time, she has been involved in supporting hundreds of people as a business trainer and coach, firstly with Truro College Business Centre, and then with Outset Cornwall.

Since 2003 she has also been working privately through 'Dare to Blossom Life Coaching' with individuals and business people around the world. Mary runs inspirational workshops and on-line programmes using all the skills she has acquired and focusing around creative visualisation using the theme of a 'Magic Carpet Ride'. She has written four books as well as creating the 'Dare to Blossom Rediscovery Cards' pack – a simple tool that promotes reflection and reconnection.

www.daretoblossom.co.uk
www.macmillan.org.uk

Kate Beddow

Diagnosed with a pituitary tumour, Kate was thankful it wasn't cancerous. But too much growth hormone had caused a rare condition called Acromegaly. Kate's humour in describing herself as Fiona from *Shrek* when her condition was at its height is testimony to her character. To get her brain working again she enrolled in a course of Spiritual Care, and now does valuable work in the classroom teaching both staff and pupils skills to maintain their emotional wellbeing.

THE PROBLEM WITH TRYING TO WRITE about a time in your life when you are in crisis is that your body goes into survival mode and it seems one of the first functions it abandons is 'record and recall'. I feel a little like a rock star from the sixties trying to recall a time in my life that, apart from a few treasured memories, is all but lost. Fortunately over the last few years I have managed to fill in a few gaps thanks to my husband and the rest of my family. Let's rewind a little to June 2004.

"I'm sorry, Mrs Beddow. Your baby hasn't grown; we're going to have to book you in for a scan."

This was the start of a very eventful journey. I was convinced everything would be ok. I had been sick for the first three months of pregnancy, but that's not unusual and, other than that, I had been very healthy: no crazy cravings or pains. Nothing out of the ordinary at all.

My first baby. I had been dreaming about being a mummy since I was a teenager and finally the moment was approaching. As I sat in the midwife's office with my husband, Ian, that morning at my thirty-four-week appointment, I never dreamt that twenty-four hours later I would be gazing with love and anxiety at my newborn.

We went for scans and monitoring the next day. She had the cord around her neck. There wasn't enough amniotic fluid around her. I would have to have an emergency caesarean that afternoon. I had no idea exactly what that involved, as I had been determined to have as natural a birth as possible. But now wasn't the time to worry about that; we just had to make sure our unborn baby was ok. At 5pm we went down to the operating theatre. A very traumatic half hour followed, with three different people trying to get an epidural into my spine. Not good for someone who is needle-phobic.

None of that mattered when they held my tiny baby next to my face for the first time. "She's so tiny" was all I could say to a distressed Ian. That brief touch was all we got before she was rushed off to the special care baby unit. The cord had indeed been wrapped around her neck, her heart had stopped every time I had a contraction and once she was here they discovered she had been passing her red blood cells back through the umbilical cord into me so she was frighteningly anaemic. She wouldn't have survived the night had she not been born when she was.

We were in shock.

Three days later we were home. Laura had had a blood transfusion and had to have iron supplements, but other than that she was small but healthy. She may have only been 4lb 3.5oz but she had 'fighter' written through her like a stick of rock. The determination and courage in that small frame was incredible.

The first few weeks weren't all sunshine and flowers though. With hindsight, I probably had a touch of postnatal depression. Laura had to feed every two hours because her tummy was so small, it didn't hold much and she had terrible reflux. Sleep was something I couldn't even dream about. I was exhausted and it didn't get any easier when she reached a healthy weight. Laura slept badly until she started school, so when I was constantly tired and started to ache all over it was logical to assume that it was due to sleep deprivation. And that's what I did. Likewise, when my feet became swollen and I went up a couple of shoe sizes, I deduced that it was because I wasn't getting to put them up as often as I should and when I put on weight, generally, I put it down to baby weight and turning thirty.

I can be quite stubborn and don't easily admit to struggling, so I continued to do all that I could to keep on top of looking after Laura, the house and the little girl I was child-minding who was a little younger than Laura.

Ian had started a full-time degree when Laura was three months old and was doing that alongside running his own business, working as a freelance sports commentator, playing guitar in a band and helping his dad with his business. You can imagine how tired we both were. I was effectively a single parent to a two-year-old and, weekdays, to an 18-month-old. Ian was working every hour of the day. We weren't functioning as a family at all by this point. We barely saw each other and we were both exhausted. Despite these pressures and demands on our time, we loved each other and had always wanted to have another baby. As Laura turned two, we decided to start trying. I became pregnant with Laura the second month of trying, so I didn't think it would be difficult.

I should just mention at this point that, when Ian and I first moved in together our beautiful friend and clairvoyant, Lisa Williams, gave me a reading. Among other things, she had told me that I would have two children – a girl and a boy – but that there would be lots of tests surrounding having a baby. At the time, it had worried me a little, but then when I became pregnant with Laura within two months of us getting married, I figured she had maybe got this little detail wrong. After all, I believe we are all in control of our own fate. Maybe I had changed my destiny at some point.

I came off the pill and my period didn't start. I waited and waited. After three months I went to the doctor. He informed me that he could only help if I went another three months without a period, and if that were to be the case, I wasn't to worry; he would refer me to the hospital and they would give me an injection that would 'switch me back on.' Not the kindest or most subtle thing to say to a hormonal and exhausted young woman!

So I waited.

During my 'waiting' time Ian finally gave in and went to the doctor about his tiredness and depression. I had known since we first met that he periodically stopped breathing while he was asleep. It scared me. I would regularly be on the brink of hitting him to bring him round when he would cough and splutter back into action. I had read about sleep apnoea, when the throat muscles relax and cause the breath to pause, a few years before and mentioned it to him, but he had dismissed it and carried on as usual. This time, however, he went to hospital, did a sleep test and discovered that he had the highest apnoea rate in Stafford. He was having over one hundred apnoeas an hour and each apnoea was an average of twenty seconds. He was seriously oxygen deprived as he was not breathing for longer than he was breathing and the specialists couldn't believe he hadn't had a heart attack or a stroke.

He was banned from driving until they could get his apnoea rate down. This was more than an inconvenience given how much we were juggling already and I was starting to think that stress may have been causing my 'ladies' problems.' Whilst Ian was a different person for getting better quality of sleep with his breathing apparatus and for accepting his depression, I still didn't have any news from my doctor. So, that Christmas I went back to the doctor and he referred me to the hospital.

Over the next four or five months I was sent from department to department for blood test after blood test and was eventually sent for an MRI. I went to see the consultant to find out the results. "Mrs Beddow, you have a pituitary tumour." I didn't hear anything else he said. I rang Ian as I walked home from the hospital and sobbed.

Was it cancerous? What were they going to do? Why was it there? I didn't know anything. Once I had composed myself, I rang the hospital and asked some questions. I had a pituitary tumour and it wasn't cancerous; it meant I was producing too much growth hormone and my cortisol levels were high.

I had a condition called acromegaly.

Remember 'Jaws' from the Bond films? The actor of giant physical proportions with height to match? He is probably the most recognisable sufferer.

For the first time in my life I was faced with something I couldn't do anything about. I didn't know what was going to happen next. Once the initial shock passed, I knew one thing: it wasn't going to beat me. My daughter was only two and there was no way I was leaving her. She needed me. Ian needed me.

Over the coming weeks I got to know my doctor very well, as I visited to ask more and more questions: would my feet return to their original size? Would I be able to have more children? Would I be in pain forever? And so many more. The prognosis wasn't good. My feet and hands wouldn't return to their true size, I wouldn't be able to have more children unless I went through IVF and, yes, I would be in pain for the rest of my life. The surgery, an endoscopic transsphenoidal hypophysectomy – I memorised it because they are such fabulous words! – may not have any impact on my condition at all. There was only a forty to sixty percent chance of it making any difference to my symptoms.

The next few months were tough. I was coping with increasing levels of pain and, despite going up four shoe sizes, two dress sizes and six ring sizes, I was still in denial. I was certainly not going to let anyone else know I was struggling. So I battled on.

In the summer of 2007, I stopped child-minding and spent all my time with Laura. By the time I went into hospital on 6 November, I had all my Christmas presents bought and wrapped and all my Christmas cards written. I made sure I had seen everyone I loved and had even written a jokey email to my friend Lisa – who by now was living in the US – letting her know what was happening and how scared I was, but also laughing about the fact that I would at least be able to keep in touch with her if the worst happened. The weekend before I went into hospital I went shopping with my sister in Leeds. Laura needed new wellies. It was the last thing on my list, and I wanted some quality time with my sister before I went into hospital.

"Right, so Laura needs new wellies. Are we just looking for plain red ones? Cheap and cheerful?" Jen asked.

"No," I replied, "we're looking for special ones. Maybe Peppa Pig, or Cinderella – they are her favourites. This might be the last pair of wellies I buy for her, I want her to remember them."

I burst into tears in the middle of the shop. It all hit me at once. I am so well practised at being practical and getting things done in a crisis, which is good, it has saved me lots of times in the past, but suddenly the severity of the situation dawned on me. It was terrifying. I was going into hospital. They were going to put me to sleep and I might not wake up. They were operating on the very centre of my brain.

It was around this time that my Gran, who I had always been very close to, had a mini-meltdown too. Whilst talking to my Dad, she broke down and asked what would happen if I was brain damaged. Somewhere in all the madness of the previous few months no one had told her that they operate through the nose for the majority of pituitary surgery and, fortunately, my tumour was at the front of my pituitary gland, so that was the method they would be using. My poor Gran thought they were going to have to shave my head and saw the top off, I think.

I was incredibly fortunate. The world's leading pituitary surgeon at that time was Dr Johnson, who just happened to be based at the hospital in Birmingham that I had been referred to. This man changed my life. He performed the surgery on 7th November 2007, my Grandma Mary's eighty- seventh birthday.

Within hours of the surgery, my body began to react. Dr Johnson did his rounds and declared that the operation had been as successful as he could have imagined. Before I even left the hospital I began to see and feel changes in my body.

The next few weeks were tough. It was hard enough in hospital, as the only evidence I had of my surgery was a small swab, my 'snot rag', which was taped under my nose. I didn't look like I'd had major surgery and I was young compared to most of the other patients who were there for hearing aids to be fitted etc, so they were constantly asking me to get things for them, which I did, gladly. It wasn't until I tried to find a lady's slipper for her under her bed, without being able to put my head down, that I was asked what I was in for. I think she was upset when I told her, but I was fine and happy to help if I could.

I tend to recover from surgery fairly quickly, but even I have to admit that this one knocked me sideways. I spent five weeks sitting on my parents' sofa in Leeds, barely able to walk to the kitchen to make a drink. I missed Laura and Ian terribly, but I wasn't able to look after Laura because I wasn't allowed to bend down and she didn't understand how delicate I was. Also, even catching a cold from a pre-schooler after having major surgery up my nose would have been really dangerous, so, I had to be careful. November is not a good time to be avoiding getting a cold! By the end of my convalescence I had gone down three shoe sizes, at least one dress size and my rings were spinning on my fingers. I had to go shopping before I could travel home because I couldn't keep my shoes on or my trousers up.

This seems like an 'and they all lived happily ever after' exit point, doesn't it? But in many ways this was just the beginning of my journey. From here on things got really interesting.

The six months following my surgery were eventful to say the least. We had an amazing family Christmas, and my friend Lisa had come over to visit from the US. She invited us to stay with her in Los Angeles for a holiday to help my recovery. Everything seemed to be perfect. And before we knew it, we were having a life-changing holiday in the US with a dear friend, who helped us to unlock this new chapter in our lives.

We had only been back from this incredible trip for a few weeks when I discovered that I was pregnant. It was quite a shock. Not only had I spent the last few years being told I couldn't have any more children, I had pretty much resigned myself to the fact that I wasn't supposed to either. The universe knew better though and, less than six months after my miraculous surgery, I was back at the doctors sharing my news. The medical professionals were more than a little surprised and had me on regular observations.

All the way through the pregnancy they told me that I wouldn't be able to have a natural birth and that I wouldn't be able to breastfeed this time because my body wouldn't produce the right levels of the right hormones required. Well, they were right about the birth. My little angel went overdue by two weeks and they wouldn't let me wait any longer. I tried everything: I ate pineapple until my tongue was sore, had acupuncture, hot curries, the lot. He was way too comfy in there. Had I not had any medical complications myself, I may have asked to wait a few more days, but, given my history, and after everything that had happened with Laura, I wasn't taking any chances.

Daniel was born weighing 7lb 15oz on the 16th January 2009. From the moment he was born, I knew my life had changed. Up until that point I was enjoying selling children's books. I was even booking school fairs the day before he was born, but the instant he arrived I knew I was destined for something else, something more. Things were so different with Daniel; he was born by caesarean but it was so calm I was laughing and joking with the nurses and midwife while they inserted the epidural. I held him as soon as he was born and hardly let him go for the first week! Ian even cut the cord. Advice had changed, so he slept in with me, which was heaven. He was beautiful. I knew instantly that my family was complete. I had my beautiful princess and my cheeky monkey and I was happy.

I had taken maternity leave from selling children's books and by now had little intention of going back to it, other than to fulfil the commitments I had already made to people. For the first time in about six years I had total control of my own head and body. I had gone from pregnant, to ill, to pregnant, with very little time to recover in between and now it was time to reclaim my brain. I didn't know what to do. I asked the angels to guide me, by now I had fully embraced my spirituality again and got up to speed through some voracious reading like a woman possessed! I needed to be shown the right direction for me to turn.

I decided to find a distance learning course that I could do while Daniel slept. By now Laura had started school, so, whatever I chose to do, it had to fit between school runs. I literally typed 'distance learning courses' into the search engine. I didn't know what else to put. I didn't know what sort of course I wanted to do. Did I want a vocational course that would lead to a job or just something fun to help me get my brain working again? One of the first courses I found was an Institute of Counselling Course called 'Spiritual Care'. It was about helping people, psychology, religion, spirituality, healing. It was perfect! I signed up there and then. Daniel was two or three weeks old by this point and he would sleep in his Moses basket next to me while I sat on the bed in my office which doubled as the spare room in those days, covered in books and papers, with a cup of herbal tea. I loved it. I have always loved learning and it felt so good to be using my intellectual brain again.

When Daniel was a year old I finally went for the follow-up scan that I should have had six months after my surgery. It showed that there was a little of the tumour remaining and the consultant recommended that I start having a low dose injection in order to keep my hormones at a healthy level.

I was reluctant to accept the injections as, in the time since my surgery, I had studied many complementary therapies and was now also a Reiki Master. I felt I could keep on top of any health issues myself. More of an issue was that it meant having to stop breastfeeding my little boy; yes, I could breastfeed too! But I reconciled myself with the fact that he'd had thirteen months of comfort and nourishment, and it was nearly time anyway. The week before my first injection he decided he had had enough, so I needn't have worried.

As reluctant as I was to have any drugs, with hindsight it was the right choice. As a mum, you rarely prioritise what your body needs and I am glad that with a simple, low dose injection every six weeks I am able to live a normal, healthy life and be the mum I want to be to my children.

I am grateful every day for my children who both helped me through this difficult time in their own magical ways; for my husband and the rest of my family, who continue to love and support me, and remind me to put my feet up when I get stubborn and forget that chronic fatigue isn't something you can ignore!

Most of all I am grateful for the perspective that all of this has given me. I feel truly fortunate to be alive, every day. I have been given opportunities and discovered career choices that I never knew existed. I've even made a few up because I felt there was a need!

Having spent years teaching in my twenties, I am now back in schools, using all my skills to help teachers and students to stay calm, happy and healthy, and help them to cope with the enormous pressures placed on them in the education system. I feel so fortunate to be able to help others and use the perspective I gained from this experience, as well as many other life experiences, to help others and improve the quality of their lives.

Everything happens for a reason, and I am grateful for all the pain, the worry and the challenges, because without those, I wouldn't have the amazing life I have now.

Biography

Having trained as a primary school teacher and worked in all ages from early years to high school, Kate made a life changing decision in 2007 after being diagnosed with a pituitary tumour. Diagnosed with a lifelong condition, and having a young daughter at the time, Kate made the decision not to return to teaching but to learn how to keep herself mentally and physically healthy using energy healing, mindfulness and relaxation techniques.

Based in the Midlands but a Yorkshire lass at heart Kate was born and raised in Leeds but has lived in Stafford since she met her husband in 2001 and now calls it home. Against all odds, Kate now has two children and runs her own holistic therapy business. She also works with schools to help them give their staff and students the skills they need to maintain their own emotional well-being. By combining her teaching and holistic skills Kate has created classes and training to help teachers help their students, and themselves, stay happy, healthy and calm.

www.katebeddow.com
www.facebook.com/groups/acrogirlsonly

Louisa

Chronic, at times life-threatening asthma and frequent hospital visits made Louisa acutely aware of the fragility of life, causing depression and loss of will to live. She battled through and achieved a Bachelor of Music degree – a testimony to her passion for music. I love the fact that a woman with severe respiratory problems chooses to play the flute. Louisa finds her teaching work with children who have additional needs both hugely rewarding and humbling.

IT ALL STARTED WHEN I WAS about eleven years old. I would frequently suffer from shortness of breath, feeling like a heavy weight was on my chest. Sometimes I was so breathless that I couldn't speak. My mother, who was not renowned for her sympathetic attitude to health problems, seemed unconcerned, and so I went about my school life as always. However, the shortness of breath continued; I struggled to participate in PE at school, barely managing one lap of the running track during lessons. After many months of worsening symptoms and several visits to my doctor, I was referred to the local hospital for further tests. I had a wide variety of allergy tests, most of which came back positive, and also a spirometry test. This involved breathing into a mouthpiece attached to a machine which then calculates how much air you can breathe out. I was diagnosed with asthma and given a blue 'reliever' inhaler that I was told to take when I became short of breath. Asthma is a condition where the airways of the lungs narrow in response to a wide variety of triggers such as allergens, the common cold, infections etc. They never really knew why my asthma was triggered but it's quite common for asthma to appear during childhood.

At this point I managed my symptoms with my blue inhaler and worked hard at school. I loved music and was learning to play the piano. I went on to study GCSE's and later, A-level music. As the years passed, I began to require more and more treatment for my asthma in order to keep my symptoms under control.

At the age of eighteen, I was lucky enough to gain a place at Edinburgh University to study a Bachelor of Music degree. After leaving home in the North of England and moving to Edinburgh to study, my symptoms became extremely difficult to manage. I was taking around six different medications a day to try and control my asthma and by the age of nineteen I'd had my first hospital admission.

During my first admission to hospital I was kept in for a couple of nights for treatment with steroids, which helped to reduce the inflammation in my lungs. I was also given a nebuliser to inhale a fine mist through a mask to open up the constricted airways. After several months I began to have an increasing number of severe attacks, all requiring hospital treatment. I also began needing more and more emergency courses of steroids. Unfortunately, the hospital admissions continued to increase and I needed emergency treatment for my asthma around every four-six weeks.

It was at this point I was officially diagnosed with 'brittle asthma', a form of asthma which is difficult to control and which features repeated life-threatening attacks. My asthma had taken on a different form. I could be fine one minute and then struggling to breathe and needing immediate treatment in Accident and Emergency. During my attacks my CO2 (Carbon Dioxide) level would rise, which is a sign that the lungs aren't able to breathe out adequately. When CO2 levels begin to rise, it is a sign that the patient's body isn't coping anymore. During one admission they had to ventilate me by putting a tube down my throat and into my lungs, it took over my breathing in order to save my life.

Living away from my family was really difficult. I felt very alone during my time at university. It wasn't that I didn't have friends, but as I was unwell so much of the time, people would gradually stop asking me to spend time with them. I would be forgotten when it came to party invitations because people would just assume I would be too sick to attend. I guess you find out who your true friends are when you are experiencing difficult times in your life. I had a couple of great friends who would drop what they were doing and come to the hospital to visit me. I was also privileged to have had the most amazing flatmate in the world. She would visit me in hospital, bring me clean clothes, take away my dirty laundry, laugh with me and cry with me. I wouldn't have survived university without her. Harriet and I are still best friends to this day and although she lives in London we regularly speak on the phone, visit each other and we also go on holiday together every summer. I couldn't ask for a more wonderful friend.

During my time at university, I struggled to cope psychologically. I was trying to keep up with my studies, have some semblance of a social life, which wasn't easy, and also cope with repeated emergency admissions to hospital. Life was becoming extremely challenging. I was then diagnosed with depression and was referred to the Liaison Psychiatry Department at the Royal Infirmary of Edinburgh. They work with patients who have psychological difficulties associated with acute and chronic health conditions. As my asthma became more severe I was frequently admitted to the High Dependency Unit or Intensive Care. As a young woman without much life experience, these wards were very scary places to be. I was witnessing things that other people my age would never have had to face; for example; hearing staff carry out CPR on the person in the next bed followed by their grieving relatives coming in to see their body. There was only a curtain between us, so I could hear everything that was being said. It was utterly terrifying. I struggled to cope with these experiences and also with my own mortality.

During this time, I met a young woman also suffering with brittle asthma. She had a very similar story to mine. We met up several times and supported each other over the phone. We would speak almost every day and I was so grateful to have someone in the same position as me to whom I could relate. Sadly, at the age of twenty-four, she passed away from a severe asthma attack. I was devastated. I was grieving for my friend but at the same time I was also acutely aware of how serious my condition was. Each time I was admitted with a severe attack I would think "Is this it? Am I going to die this time?" It was a very dark time for me.

I carried on seeing my liaison psychiatrist. Along with my doctors, she was concerned that I wasn't taking my medications regularly. I wasn't. I had mentally given up on life. I felt "What's the point? I'll die anyway just like my friend." I was suffering from a very depressed state of mind and it was during this time that I began antidepressant therapy.

The respiratory team at the hospital decided to give me a nebuliser to use at home. The medication helped to dilate my narrowed airways. Patients usually only receive nebuliser treatment in hospital but I had now been issued the machine to use at home in an attempt to reduce the number of my emergency admissions to hospital. I carried it everywhere I went in the case of an asthma attack.

The night times in hospital were the worst. Asthma is usually at it's worst in the early hours of the morning and life seems more negative during those early hours. When it's dark outside and you feel like every single breath is a huge effort, your mind starts to really wander. Being in hospital was also quite disturbing at times. There was far too much time to think about life, to worry about what might be. I was often lying awake when patients on the respiratory ward passed away during the night. The curtains would be drawn around our beds and you could hear the rattling of the metal mortuary trolley coming to take the patient away. No sooner had the bed been remade and another patient was admitted into the same bed. It was very strange to me how the hospital continued to function like a well-oiled machine, dead patient out, new patient in. It seemed cold and uncaring, but life carried on. It made me more aware of the fragility of life, of how close we all are to the edge. Whilst my university friends were out partying I was lying in a hospital bed contemplating life, death and everything in between. It was a stark contrast.

By my fourth year at university I was in hospital more than ever. I remember having fourteen admissions during that year. I was studying for my Honours Degree, juggling numerous medications, trying to cope with frequent admissions to hospital and also struggling with depression. In a last ditch attempt to keep me out of hospital I was started on a Terbutaline syringe driver. This delivered a constant dose of Terbutaline underneath my skin. Terbutaline is a bronchodilator which helps the air passages in the lungs to open up. This really helped to restore me with some quality of life at the time but unfortunately it meant I was attached to the machine about the size of a pencil case and I wore it on a belt around my waist for twenty-four hours a day. Every few days I had to go to the doctor's surgery to get the needle taken out and a new one put in. I had the most fantastic practice nurse, Helen, who changed all my needles and accompanied me to hospital when I was too unwell to decide for myself. This was quite common! I would frequently get to the point where I just couldn't cope psychologically with the thought of going back in to hospital again so I needed someone else to decide for me. I must have been a nightmare patient at times. Helen gave me so much support during my years at university and I would never have survived without her.

The music department at the university were extremely supportive and understanding and would bring work into the ward for me so I could catch up. My final year was exhausting as I wrote my dissertations, studied for exams and tried to cope with my chronic health condition. In July 1999, I graduated with a Bachelor of Music with Honours. I was so happy to have achieved my degree after what had been the most difficult and extremely challenging time.

I chose to remain in Edinburgh after graduating. I was unable to work and survived solely on disability benefits. I studied for a piano recital diploma at Trinity College of Music, London. This was assessed by a final recital at the end of the year, so it meant I could practice as and when I was able to. After passing my recital diploma I decided I wanted to go into music teaching, as I really wanted to work with children who have 'additional support needs.' I was told I was crazy!

"How would I cope with my health being so poor? What if I caught infections from the children? What about my syringe driver? How would I use my nebuliser at work?"

I was so determined! I couldn't think of a better person to work with children who have additional needs than someone who has, themselves, struggled with adversity. I knew I had something to offer.

My first few months of my PGCE music went well. We mainly studied different teaching approaches and curriculum. Then came my first teaching placement. I remember taking my teaching mentor to one side and explaining to him that I may at some point need to use my nebuliser and not to be alarmed if they saw me attached to a machine with a mask on my face! I always think it's wise to share this with people before the event, in case something happens and they panic and call an ambulance. I use a nebuliser every day as part of my treatment so it's no big deal for me, but I understand it can look a bit scary to other people!

I managed to get through all three placements without using my nebuliser in front of people. I occasionally went into to the toilet cubicle to do a treatment, not very classy, but it's less dramatic to do it in private. People tend to freak out sometimes if they're not used to seeing it. I had a few admissions to hospital during my teacher training, but in general my emergency admissions were less frequent and I was managing to control most of my symptoms myself, albeit with a hefty dose of medication.

Towards the end of my teacher training, I went for my routine medical, it's something all student teachers need to have before they can become a fully registered teacher with the General Teaching Council. I failed my medical.

Words cannot explain how devastated I was. I had worked so hard, only for them to tell me I wasn't 'fit to teach'.

But I had been teaching! I'd been teaching every day on my placement. I was doing well and had received 'A's' and 'B's' for my teaching assessments. How could they tell me I wasn't 'fit to teach?' I'd only had a couple of days off sick during the entire year. They were judging me on the amount of treatment I was taking and also by what my lungs sounded like on the day they examined me. They didn't speak to my colleagues and find out whether this affected my ability to do the job that I was trained for. In fact, many of the staff I was on placement with didn't even know about my condition as I had managed to be so discreet when requiring and administering my treatment. I wasn't going to throw away all of my training and sit at home being a sick person for the rest of my life. I appealed against their decision and was summoned for a second medical, which I also failed! Eventually my respiratory consultant and my course tutor provided evidence that I could, and indeed was, doing my teaching job to a high standard, regardless of my medical condition. They reversed the decision and declared me 'fit to teach'. Success! Finally, I could have the career I had trained for and wanted so much.

In 2003 I married my partner, whom I had met at university when I was eighteen. Life was good. I was starting out life as a newlywed and I finally had some control over my brittle asthma.

I was keen to come off my syringe driver, mainly because it was annoying having to carry it around and get the needles changed all the time. I also wanted to have a more 'normal' life and being connected to a tube and a pump every day was a constant reminder of my condition. Shortly after I was married I went into hospital to get weaned off the infusion pump and it was successful.

After a number of teaching jobs spanning several years, I eventually gained my current post where I have taught for the past eleven years, working as a music teacher with children who are blind or partially sighted. Many of the pupils, in addition to their visual impairment also have complex physical and cognitive impairments.

On embarking upon my career, I was always very keen that I wanted my colleagues to know me as a professional and not simply as someone with a chronic health condition. During university I had often felt like my health condition dominated my life so much that I had lost who I really was. Of course, most of the staff at work know that I'm in hospital every now and again. Some of them know about my brittle asthma but that's ok. It doesn't define me anymore. There is so much more to me than my chronic health condition.

Sadly, in 2013, my marriage ended after my husband admitted having an affair. To say I was devastated would be an understatement. After almost ten years of marriage I couldn't believe that it was all over.

This was an extremely difficult time for me. I was mourning the loss of my husband and my marriage and I was also terrified about managing on my own. During this time my depression came back with an intense ferocity. I needed therapy to help me cope with the feelings and emotions that were coming up. I felt scared, rejected and ashamed. Yes, I felt ashamed. Ashamed that my husband felt the need to start a relationship with another woman. I wasn't good enough. If I had been a 'good enough' wife he wouldn't have had an affair. Looking back I now know that this is a common feeling amongst spouses who have suffered infidelity. Several years later I now understand that it wasn't my fault and that I couldn't have been responsible for his actions.

I moved out of the marital home, and into a new house. This was the first time I had bought a house without him at my side and it was really scary, but I did it! I had my own home and from this starting point I began to slowly rebuild my life.

Today I have a good quality of life. I have many friends and an active social life. I play percussion in an orchestra and I go tap dancing once a week. I have tentatively begun dating again and my current relationship seems quite promising. I often keep my emotions well hidden when I'm in a relationship because I'm scared of being hurt again. It's difficult to trust men when you have been hurt in the past but I am trying to slowly become more and more trusting when it comes to sharing my feelings and emotions.

I still have regular therapy as I find that it helps me to cope with my depression and also gives me much needed support in managing the day-to-day demands of my health condition.

My asthma currently remains relatively stable, although it can be quite difficult to manage alongside a professional career and the practicalities of daily life. At work, I sometimes lock the classroom door to use my nebuliser in private, other times I nip into a toilet cubicle for a quick inhale when I'm feeling wheezy. I struggle with catching colds, a common theme amongst most teachers, even the healthy ones! Colds and other viruses often result in a deterioration to my health that I have to be admitted to hospital, so I have to be really careful. I'm in hospital around once or twice a year now. The rest of my time I manage my condition myself at home.

I love my teaching job. My work involves using alternative methods to communicate with pupils through the medium of sound, moving beyond their sensory and cognitive impairments and finding ways in which music can be used to communicate where other approaches have previously failed. I never tire of being excited by the responses that music can evoke in children with additional support needs. It might be that a child makes a small vocal sound in response to your voice, or that they move their hand slightly to feel the vibration of a musical instrument. It is the most rewarding job I could ask for and I feel so humbled every day to have been given the opportunity to work with these wonderful children.

In recent years, I have cultivated a more caring attitude towards myself and my body. I have learned to listen to my body in order to understand it and care for it. Rather than simply trying to 'push through' my symptoms, which inevitably doesn't work. I will go for a lie down or increase/adjust my medication. Sometimes this will also mean cancelling my plans in order to take care of myself, but I know that if I try to keep going when I'm unwell then it will backfire and I will end up in hospital again. I give my chronic condition the respect that it deserves and this, in turn, has led to a more balanced life both physically and psychologically. I used to get so angry and frustrated at my health condition but I now accept that brittle asthma is just one part of my life and rather than trying to fight against it I now accept it as part of who I am. Sometimes life can get difficult and tiring, managing my chronic condition and working full time, but I wouldn't change it for the world. Life is good!

Biography

Louisa has recently undertaken further academic study to enable her to become a Qualified Teacher of the Visually Impaired (QTVI), also achieving qualifications in the reading and writing of Braille.

In her free time Louisa practices meditation and enjoys taking time out to relax through regular walks in the beautiful Scottish landscape. A music lover by heart, Louisa enjoys both performing and listening to a wide variety of music. She plays the piano to unwind and is also a Percussionist for Edinburgh Concert Band, who perform in a range of concerts throughout the year.

Louisa is an animal lover and in spite of her asthma will spend endless amounts of time giving her attention to anything fluffy! She recently acquired a kitten – a Siberian Forest cat, which are known to be hypoallergenic because their saliva contains lower levels of the protein responsible for cat allergies. So far, so good! Most of all, Louisa enjoys spending valuable time with friends and catching up with them over a good cuppa, or perhaps even a glass or two of Prosecco.

www.asthma.org.uk

Laura Steckler

Laura's love affair with dance and movement has lasted her entire life. Accepting a place into a doctoral programme in clinical psychology at the age of twenty-four was not her first choice, but she was happily able to dance as well as study. An injury and doctor's advice put an end to her dancing, and at times she could barely walk. Her long and painful journey has led her to helping others with chronic pain. Her beautiful, liberated movements were not easy to capture as she moved so fast and with such graceful freedom!

> Here is an amazement – once I was twenty years old
> and in every motion of my body there was a delicious ease,
> and now I am sixty years old, and it is the same.
>
> Mary Oliver

> Once a Dancer, always a Dancer
>
> Dr Laura Hope Steckler

MOVEMENT WAS MY FIRST LOVE. I used to spin around on the grass as a child until I fell dizzily to the ground with my head happily spinning, smelling the fragrant freshly cut grass. I began ballet at four but my mother, concerned about the brutality of toe shoes, made me stop. I continued to be involved with creative movement and Dalkroze Eurythmics classes. However, as teenage hormones took over I lost interest. Then, just after completing my university degree in psychology, I fell in love with dance all over again. I was particularly drawn to sensuality and the organic nature of contemporary dance and release-based techniques. I started taking one class a week. My teacher Lesley Woideck said "You need to dance every day if you want to be a dancer".

And so, I increased my classes to two, then three a week. I began to practice pliés, relevés and movement combinations at home.

My mother, with whom I had a challenging relationship, was not always supportive of my dancing. She had her own frustrations and misgivings about dance. However, something she once said really stuck with me: "Once a dancer, always a dancer". My love affair with dance and movement has lasted my entire life, till today, at the age of sixty-five.

After falling back in love with dance I had a dilemma, I had been accepted into a doctoral programme in Clinical Psychology. This was no mean feat, as they say, as only ten percent of applicants get a place. Should I follow my heart or do the practical thing? I had been offered a scholarship at the University of South Carolina, so that I didn't have to pay tuition fees. This was hard to turn down. In addition, although I was only twenty-four years old, I thought I was 'too old' to be a dancer. So, I ultimately opted for the safe route of psychology.

Nonetheless, it was during my doctoral programme that I did my first performing and choreography! I choreographed and performed a group piece called 'Wind Danse' to music by Chic Corea. I had room for little else in my life, consumed by writing papers, reading, attending both psychology and dance classes. I was so thrilled that I was able to dance as well as do my doctoral degree. My whole doctoral student class came to see me perform and cheered me on.

One day during a ballet class I was doing an arabesque, a movement where the leg is lifted and extended behind the body. I felt a sudden searing pain in my back. I could barely move. I remember leaning up against the wall to try to ease my pain feeling bewildered and in shock. I subsequently had severe shooting pain down my leg and into my foot. It was difficult to sleep because any movement triggered this excruciating pain, which over the counter painkillers did little to alleviate.

I saw a specialist orthopaedic doctor, who took x-rays of my spine. I will never forget the day that he showed me those x-rays. He had a group of students with him. He introduced me to them "This is Laura. She is a dancer, well she WAS a dancer".

He proceeded to show me that one of my vertebrae was fractured in two places, probably congenitally. I had a condition called 'Spondylolysis'. This condition leads to instability of the spine and irritation of the sciatic nerve, which runs from the spine down the leg and into the foot. He said, "Whatever you do, don't arch your back. If you don't do what I tell you I will put you in the hospital in traction". He said that if I wasn't careful my vertebra could slip (spondylolisthesis) and cause spinal cord damage.

This cruel and misguided information haunted me for years. I now know that our bodies are meant to move in all directions. The muscles surrounding the spine can support the spine and prevent slippage. Yes, I needed to be cautious but the fear of movement he instilled in me was totally unnecessary. I was afraid to move the wrong way for fear of damaging my spinal cord. The edict to not arch my back meant that I was restricting my movement and thereby creating stiffness and unnatural movement patterns that created additional pain problems.

I was in frequent intense pain, at times shooting, burning or numbness (numbness is actually a type of pain called 'neuropathic pain'). I was on constant anti-inflammatory medication. At times, I could barely walk. I went to see chiropractors, which only seemed to make things worse. I consulted other doctors, one of whom told me to have surgery. I considered this but did not want to go under the knife. Another one, looking at my x-rays said, "You are in great shape, you are beautiful, but you are over the hill". I was twenty-eight!

I then saw another doctor, this time a physiatrist (physical medicine specialist) who was also a dancer. She supported the possibility of getting back to dancing. She told me that I should think of myself as an 'old lady' and start walking for five minutes at a time and build up gradually. Although the 'old lady' image was not particularly helpful, starting small and building up gradually has been instrumental to my ability to expand my activities. It was horribly frustrating to walk such a short period of time at first. I also had to pace my activities, deciding whether I would do my laundry or shop for groceries on a given day; I could not do both. But very, very gradually I was able to do more and more.

In my search for things that would help me to be able to dance again I discovered the Alexander Technique, a method that assists in postural education and realignment, and the Feldenkrais Method®, another method that uses small micro-movements to help the body find the most efficient way of aligning itself and moving. I learned that I needed core strength to compensate for the instability in my spine. I attended physiotherapy for several months, two to three times per week. I did Pilates. I did daily meditations lying on my back in which I visualised my spine being well. I did Yoga and had one to one sessions with a Yoga teacher named John Friend. Although not a religious person, I prayed! Call me stubborn, crazy, or obsessed, I did not give up. I tried just about everything.

All these practises taught me to listen deeply to my body and how it wanted to move and when it wasn't happy with a pattern of movement. Eventually, having enough core strength and having improved my alignment, I was able to attend dance classes and do more dance movement. I was still using medication and needed regular massage and strict self-care to manage my pain. By now I was in my early thirties. I had moved to Houston Texas to do my internship in Clinical Psychology at the world-famous Texas Medical Center. After completing my internship and still working on my Doctoral Dissertation I decided to commence a Master's degree in dance. I was also working as a Clinical Psychologist. Again, my life was consumed by these activities and did not leave room for much else!

My back problems waxed and waned. I had another major setback after doing a year of my M.A. in dance. I had hoped to join one of the local dance companies in Houston but this was not to be, I was in too much pain. Nonetheless, I persisted in exploring somatic (body) methods and maintaining my core strength and moved as much as I could.

I was completing my doctorate and grateful that I was able to do something that did not aggravate my back. But the call of dance whispered to me daily. I felt I needed to do something creative so began to take acting classes and did some theatre performances and two television commercials. Though I enjoyed these experiences, the call of movement still tugged at my heart. So, I began to create my own movement performance work, which allowed me to work within my own limits. I made two pieces that were performed at the Houston International Festival, one a solo and another a group piece that I directed but did not perform in. Still I struggled with pain and limitation of movement.

In my forties, I learned of a woman who had synthesised my three loves: The Alexander Technique, the Feldenkrais Method® and Gestalt Therapy. Her name was Ilana Rubenfeld. When I went to the Omega Institute in Upstate New York to take a five-day workshop with her, I was so excited! Rubenfeld's work brought together my love of body awareness, movement, and psychotherapy into an amazingly effective, creative and fruitful package. I had enjoyed my work as a Clinical Psychologist to an extent but it did not feel like it was completely 'me'. The Rubenfeld work brought an artistry and body focus to my work, which felt like the missing link.

I went on to train with Ilana Rubenfeld In New York's Greenwich Village. She is widely considered to be a pioneer in the field of Body-Oriented Psychotherapy. She is a quirky, brilliant native New Yorker. She was in her sixties at the time I trained with her and had more energy and vitality than many people half her age.

Rubenfeld was originally a musician and had studied orchestral conducting at Julliard. She had her own back problems, which were the impetus for her to develop her work. During my training with her, I learned many Feldenkrais exercises that helped my back problems as they helped me to listen very closely and deeply to my body and for my body to integrate itself more efficiently. I also learned more about the emotional factors in my back pain. Her method is called the Rubenfeld Synergy® Method.

I do not believe in a simplistic body-mind connection but do believe that emotional factors affect our physiological functioning in ways we cannot completely comprehend at present. I had some very deep and cathartic sessions during my training leading to healing on a deep level from traumatic events in my early life.

Around that time, I began dancing again. A real achievement was performing with my dear friend Sara Draper in a piece we co-choreographed in collaboration with a drummer and a group of singers. I still had pain, and the day of the performance I was in tears in the morning. I went to see my wonderful massage therapist Jana who really helped. I remember her saying, "I am going to take the pain away". And she did! As long as I warmed up properly, took my ibuprofen, stretched, and iced my back after performing, I was ok.

After competing my training with Rubenfeld I attended the first ever Body Oriented Psychotherapy conference in the USA. It was held in Beverly Massachusetts in 1996. What a buzz was happening there! There was so much excitement about the mind/body connection and the fruits that people were discovering about this. There were like-minded colleagues from all over the globe.

On the Saturday of the conference two things happened to me: firstly, I volunteered to be a 'client' for a group of attendees in a workshop with Al Pesso, another pioneer in the Body Psychotherapy field. Among the attendees were the likes of Bessel Van der Kolk (a well-known trauma researcher and author), and others. The session I had with Al was extremely powerful. The entire group was involved in my session and some participants played roles of family members in a sort of psychodrama (I think Bessel played the role of my Dad). Secondly, later that night I danced with a handsome, cheeky charming Brit. We kept in touch and he persuaded me with poetry, generosity, and love to move to the other side of the Atlantic where I now reside. He is now my husband and his love and support have also aided my healing.

This healing journey has led me to want to help others with pain. I took a job as a Clinical Psychologist in a chronic pain service in the National Health Service, at first in Edinburgh at the Astley Ainsley Hospital and then in the Scottish Borders at the Borders General Hospital. My training with Rubenfeld was influential in the work I did there. I have continued to specialise in working with people that have chronic pain and other health conditions. I also did training in mindfulness approaches, which dovetailed nicely with Rubenfeld's work, and I have integrated these approaches in my therapeutic work.

Since then I have been able to stop using anti-inflammatory medication and rarely need to use ice anymore. I did a one-woman show at the Edinburgh Festival Fringe in 2001 among a number of other performances. I could now walk, run, jump, skip and hop with delight! I directed and performed in a project entitled 'Hologram' in 2011, which was performed in Edinburgh and Glasgow and in which I *arched my back!*

In 2011 in the midst of the 'Hologram' project I faced another major setback – this time not spine related. I had what I thought was a virus which did not go away and I became weaker and weaker until I could barely speak or walk. I underwent a number of medical tests and eventually was given the diagnosis of 'Post Viral Syndrome', also known as 'Myalgic Encephalomylitis' or 'Chronic Fatigue Syndrome'.

This was devastating. However, using what I learned in my spinal journey, i.e., pacing and slow building of activity, listening to my body, meditation, visualisation etc, along with nutritional supplements I have eventually come 'back to life' and am now dancing again.

I am not dancing as much as I used to – I am very busy and satisfied with my therapeutic work and have found the pressures and stress of performance and making grant applications for these rather onerous. However, I am moving with greater agility and with less pain than I ever have. I use movement in my work and regularly attend movement improvisation classes. I am still open to possibilities. Who knows, maybe I will be in my next performance when I am 80!

Biography

Laura Hope Steckler Ph.D., C Psychol, RSMT, is a Clinical and Somatic Psychologist, Body-Psychotherapist, Somatic Movement Therapist, and Mindfulness instructor. She was born and trained in the USA and has lived in the UK for nineteen years. She trained with Body Psychotherapy pioneer Ilana Rubenfeld and is a certified Rubenfeld Synergist®. She has danced and choreographed professionally and has extensive experience with various movement and somatic disciplines and their use in clinical work.

She has a deep and abiding interest in the mind-body connection and how movement can be used to facilitate wholeness and well-being. Her chapter in the *Oxford Handbook of Dance and Well-being* (2017) is entitled 'Listening to the Moving Body: Movement Approaches in Body Psychotherapy'.

www.laura-steckler.com

Four

Death does Not Define Me

It's not how tragically we suffer but how miraculously we live.

Anon

Rachel Singers

Finding a way through the darkness of losing her mother in such a shocking and unexpected way was crushing for Rachel. At times, only the thought of her younger sister kept her going. Finding the right kind of counselling with a special support group brought deeper understanding and ultimately, healing. This lovely young woman is now passionate about helping as many as possible through the stigma surrounding mental health. She is a true credit to her beloved mother.

WHEN I HEARD THE NEWS THAT my mother had taken her own life on 9th May 2008 I honestly didn't know how I would ever survive thereafter.

You could have told me anything that day and I would have probably believed you, but not that. Not that my beautiful, kind mother had killed herself; I couldn't believe that she was gone let alone that she had actually chosen to leave us. I didn't just lose my mum that day; I lost one of my best friends and my biggest support system. It was so sudden and unexpected, and it crushed me. How could I live with the sadness, the guilt and the anger that laid heavy on my mind? I found it impossible to see a life where I could learn to be happy. I was submerged in darkness and often felt the urge to follow her. I could have become a casualty of what they call 'the domino effect,' but I knew in my heart of hearts I could never put my family through that heartache again. I have a younger sister who was only seventeen years old at that time. I felt a deep urge to stay with her and protect her. We've always had a special bond in which I doted on her. I would always be there for her if ever she needed me and she really was, and still is so special to me. During that awful time I was suffering and I was lost but knowing she was in pain was more than I could bear. I'm sure we were both terrified of losing each other. I felt so weak, like I couldn't go on, but I had to find a way to survive the pain so that my sister could survive it; so that my family could survive it too.

My mum, Lynda, was an incredibly successful, professional person who always put other people first. From the outside looking in she seemed to have everything: the house, the car, the husband, the career, family and friends. She was only forty-three and she seemed to have a fulfilling life ahead of her. Sadly, she was a silent sufferer like so many others. Losing her was so sudden and unexpected and it crushed me. After, I got the news about my mum, I had my family all around me and friends who would offer a shoulder to cry on, but I still felt so alone. Sometimes, people try not to talk about death, or about a person who has died, in fear that it will upset the bereaved. But, in fact, even though it is sad it can be a comfort to be reminded of the ones who have died. I know that this is true of me, talking about her helps to keep her character alive. Having said that, due to the circumstances surrounding my mum's death initially I found it hard to open up and talk to anyone because of the stigma surrounding suicide and ironically I didn't want to upset anyone by talking about it. Suicide is sadly still seen as a sort of blasphemy: a word we must not speak.

Some people see suicide as a shameful matter; the same often goes for mental health illness itself. It's repeatedly misunderstood. There is a saying that "If you break your arm everyone runs to sign your cast but if you have depression everyone runs the other way." You often can't see physical symptoms of depression but it doesn't make it any less serious. The truth is depression is a disease, just like cancer. Unless you get the help and treatment you need it eats away at you slowly but surely, until it eventually kills you. It's hard to see the symptoms of depression; I know all too well how easily they can be masked. Of course, I'm talking about the silent sufferers like my mother, but I'm also talking about my own personal experience. I found it easier to pretend and smile and hide beneath a sense of humour; to say, "I'm ok," rather than to speak of my pain. I sometimes wondered how people couldn't see the true sorrow in my eyes; what a great pretender I must have been. It can be an isolating world, one in which you can feel alone even when surrounded by a crowd of loved ones. It's often people who don't look like they need help and those who do not ask for help that need it the most.

I tried many approaches in an attempt to help myself heal so I could go on and live a more harmonious life. First, I went to see a counsellor after being referred by the doctor. Although it was somewhat therapeutic to talk things over I didn't gain all that much from the meetings. I felt the counsellor was telling me only what she thought I might want to hear. She couldn't possibly know what my mum was or wasn't thinking that day; she certainly couldn't comprehend how I was feeling. Hearing that it wasn't my fault and that I couldn't have changed the events of that day didn't make me believe otherwise. That's not to say I reject the idea of counselling, it most definitely has its part to play. I think you just need to find what works for you.

Seven years after my mum's death, I was still struggling when I heard of a support group specifically set up for people who had been bereaved by suicide called SOBS (Survivors of Bereavement by Suicide). I feel a huge sense of gratitude for finding them. It was there I got to meet other people who had gone through a similar experience. All of them had the same admissions of guilt, anger and sadness. They shared an understanding of my 'what ifs' and 'maybes'. When I spoke about how I felt, about how

I believed I might have been able to save her, no-one disagreed or tried to dismiss the possibility. In their minds they felt the same about the loved ones they had lost. There was a deeper understanding. They spoke more sense and understood me more than anyone else I had spoken to. Not only did they help me, but I helped them and I felt a real sense of purpose. Sharing my experiences helped others to open up; one mother who had lost her eighteen-year-old son to suicide expressed that she had been thinking about taking her own life and joining her son. But after seeing me, and hearing my story she realised she could never do that to her remaining daughter. It was so soothing to be around people who could identify with how I was feeling, and to know that I played a part in helping others to start to heal is beyond words. However, although it is an incredible group, it is painful. Sometimes I'd cry hearing of other people's pain, almost forgetting my own. The devastation of suicide really is like no other.

Besides from the support group, over the years I have mostly accredited surviving the pain of losing my mother to my dog Jasper. I got Jasper a few months before that dreaded day. Before deciding to get a dog you should know that I made a promise to myself and to him that he would be walked every single day. I knew the joy and love a dog could bring and that was the least I could do in return. Little did I know what he was about to do for me could never be repaid. He was the only one who was there for me as I needed him to be, any time of any day. He was there when I needed him and when I didn't. Jasper gave me so much purpose to continue to fight through the pain, he got me out of the house every single day no matter the weather, so there was never a day when I didn't breathe in the fresh air, and crucially, he made me laugh every day and continues to do so. I've often said that if it wasn't for Jasper I would not be here today and that may still very well be true.

However, in recent years I have come to realise that although Jasper helped me to survive, only I could help myself to live. I needed to become my own hero. Since setting up a new business in July 2016 I have immersed myself in self-development. There is a stigma around this too. I have discovered that self-development is another word for self-help. Self- development is far better fitting in my opinion though. Some of the happiest, most successful people undergo self-development every day. After all it really just means improving one's self and no one is perfect; there is always room for improvement. I have become engrossed in other people's success stories and have learned that all this time I have been acting like a victim. So many people have overcome larger obstacles than the one I was faced with, so why not me? I made a conscious choice to become more grateful for the things I have and to grow as a person each day and I can honestly say that since starting this journey of self-development I am the happiest I've ever been. I'm finally on a journey to become the best version of myself and I feel as though I am able to move forward.

In the past, grief has been viewed as a process whereby mourners withdraw from the world so that detachment from the deceased can gradually take place. The function of grief was thought to release the individual from his or her bond with the deceased, meaning the bereaved can find closure. I don't think anyone ever finds 'closure' or gets over a loss. You just learn to make peace with it and continue your bond with them even after death. I've learnt to live with what's happened as best I can and I continue my bond with my mum through objects such as photographs and personal items and my memories. I can be happy now as I know that's what she would want for me. I will succeed with everything I do because of her. She is my 'why.' If people ask me why I am reaching for my goals with no inhibitions I tell them it's because I want to make my mother proud. I'm grateful for the time I had with my mother and that I knew her, I'm grateful that I've become a stronger more positive person than ever before, and I am grateful that I have found the strength and courage to go on and help others.

Recently, I recorded a 'Facebook Live' which lasted around twenty-five minutes; this involved me sharing my story to a live audience online. Within the video I share my experiences and how I overcame various obstacles. I saw this as an opportunity to show others that is okay to speak out and share our experiences of 'suicide'. This video has been shared many times and now has over five thousand views, but more importantly I have received hundreds of messages of kindness, gratitude, and inspiration. I had hoped that if the video helped even one person I would have made a difference and it would be the start of me using my experience to help others. Some people have thanked me and expressed that I've helped them in a number of different ways. Some people were fellow survivors of bereavement by suicide and seeing me light up on screen even when talking about my darkest moments have given them hope that they can get through their roughest times. Some people expressed concern about family and friends that they knew who had been affected by suicide. In the past they explained they had been afraid to broach the subject and mention the deceased in fear of upsetting the bereaved. However, after hearing that I found it therapeutic to talk about my mother and my experience it has spurred them on to help others like me open up, eliminating the fear of upsetting them. Others reached out and simply expressed that they were in need of help and I've been there as a comfort for them. I'm so grateful for these acknowledgements as thanks to them I know that I accomplished my mission of helping one person, and many more.

In the future I hope to be a part of changing the stigma surrounding mental health. I am so passionate about sharing my story and helping as many people as possible, whether that be educating people on the truth about mental health illness's or reaching out to fellow sufferers and survivors. As a result of my mother's early passing I have made it my life mission to live every single day to the fullest as time is so precious and none of us really know how much time we have left with the people we love.

Finally, I think it's worth mentioning, I still have my days of uncertainty. Sometimes I stumble and lose my way. I'm not perfect, and I'll certainly never 'get over it'. Some days still get me down but when they do I try to go to bed knowing that tomorrow will be better. I believe your thoughts manifest. I used to go to sleep at night after a horrible day dreading the next as I felt it would be the same; I would feel the same. The next day I'd wake and it would be another horrible day just as I had predicted. Now, if I have a bad day I go to sleep knowing that tomorrow will be better; I will be better and the more positively I am able to think, the more positive things come my way. Sometimes you can't see the light at the end of a long painful tunnel, but know that it's there and it's brighter than you or I can ever imagine.

Biography

In 2004 Rachel studied a BTEC Overseas Operations with Children course sponsored by AirTours travel. She was assigned as a Children's Representative in Ibiza where her love for travel began. She completed three seasons with AirTours and in the summer of 2006 gained a position with Camp America, working at summer camps during 2006 and 2007. These experiences helped mold Rachel into the independent and outgoing individual that she is.

Rachel has always been a creative person, enjoying art and design, writing, poetry and performing. This creative urge led her to study for a degree in Ceramics in which she graduated from Cardiff Metropolitan with a BA in 2014. In 2011 Rachel met her now husband Jack Singers with whom she lives happily in their family home with their beloved dog Jasper.

www.facebook.com/rachelsingerspage
rachelsingers22@gmail.com

Sam Bawden

With music her passion, Sam set out to work in the industry, living the high life in London and Los Angeles – a rebel with a cause. Without the love or support from her father, she loved her brother dearly – he was the strong male figure in her life. Losing him ripped her to shreds. Then, losing her husband was devastating. She has rebuilt herself with sheer tenacity and guts, has discovered an inner strength, and is no longer scared of an unknown future.

I HAVE TO SAY I AM honoured to be included in this book, and do not feel justified to be selected for the first volume, but I will tell my story nonetheless. It has been a rollercoaster so far and I doubt the next few years will be any different!

Self-esteem, confidence, and belief in myself has never been easy for me but I am lucky to have been born to an amazingly supportive mother and caring family who, along with a good sense of humour, have continued to applaud my personal achievements and pick me up during my many failures. A good support network is essential for me as independence has never been important to me until the last three years when I became a single mother. This is now a new chapter for me, one which is unknown – and rather exciting on a good day! Where I will fit in this book I know not, each chapter title resonates with me.

I was born in Leicester in the sixties. I had a younger brother called Matthew and my parents divorced when I was five. My father remarried the woman he had an affair with, she was nice enough to me and I inherited two half siblings, Dylan and Bianca. I don't have many memories of my father; I think I have blocked them out, but my life with my mother and brother as a family of three more than made up for that. As a child, I was quite 'normal,' well behaved I guess – my brother was the live wire. I had no huge desire for success or achievements, I remember just wanting my mum to be happy and not alone. I got my wish when she married her boyfriend of ten years when I was in my twenties.

My father was a musician, he would say a great one, but I never played anything. I just had a passion for music like most young people do, and felt that I simply had to work in the music business. I moved to London I somehow managed to 'blag' my way into many music business jobs, through sheer exaggeration, enthusiasm and good looks at the time I guess! I partied like crazy, hung out with many celebrities of that time and dated more than my fair share of DJ's and musicians. My daily motivation usually being which showbiz party I could go to that evening. Money was never a motivation but my passion for music was. I was never happier than when I was listening to an album or at a gig or on a music video set. It was always about the art and thirty years later, it still is.

My late twenties took me further afield to Los Angeles where I lived very happily for seven years. Most of them as an 'illegal alien,' which culminated in me being deported from Miami for my sins and banned from the States. This has since been rectified, and now the USA can be graced with my presence again. I always felt at home in LA and have many good friends there; I think in another life I was a Californian beach bum, an artist, or a totally cool 'roller skater' girl, but in this lifetime I was a party animal who drank my USA counterparts under the table. I was a nanny for a wonderful family for a long time when I first arrived and later had many cool jobs including music videos, soundtrack, and music management. I also married a gay man on a beach in Carmel but more about that later!

On a personal level these early years above, although seemingly full of angst, boy dramas and hangovers, were relatively easy as youth is a time when we don't reflect, analyse or worry. I just got out there and did it. Self-doubt was not an option; I had no interest or time for it. Would I change any of the above? God no, I would live it all exactly the same. My memory is sketchy of most of my crazy moments, I blame it on tequila but fortunately (or unfortunately) my mother and friends have many memories of my crazy escapades, and when I hear them I laugh and think "I liked the girl I was back then" and feel quite proud of my younger self. She was brave and fearless, laid back and fun. That girl is still in here but a little more jaded and wrinkled perhaps, a bit battle worn but deep inside that flame still burns, it just needs some strong fanning sometimes!

I came back to the United Kingdom in my mid-thirties. Strangely the things that drove me away eventually brought me back. I missed England, its familiarity, and the English way of life and of course my family.

I must mention here I guess that my relationship with my father was not good. I found him to be utterly self-absorbed and selfish, and throughout my whole life my mother was the one I went to when I needed help or support. I struggled always with his lack of interest and I know that I suffered from many of the classic Daddy issues when a daughter has zero interest from her father. He was always competitive with me too, whatever I had done you can guarantee he had done it better. My grandfather 'Bunny' on my mother's side and my brother Matthew, 'Matt' were my strong male figures in my life and I loved them dearly. I know I harboured a lot of anger towards my father back then yet I chose to ignore it. I remember when I told him I had married a gay man, he sent me a letter belittling me, saying that "I had finally excelled myself in my mission to find a truly unavailable man". That hurt. At the time, I truly thought I had found a new best friend, he was good to me, we laughed all the time and he loved shopping! What's not to love? Of course, it didn't end well, he ended up in the Betty Ford Clinic and I ran home to England to nurse my broken heart. Six months later I met him in Hong Kong for a reunion but of course it didn't work out. We got divorced and that was that.

When I came back to England I started working for a company that organised Cheltenham Jazz Festival and the Ross-on-Wye International Festival. I loved this role so much. Working with musicians and seeing so many artistic performances in many genres including dance and music made my soul soar. My bosses Helen Wragg and Jim Smith were so inspirational to me, they worked so hard for the community and their artistic visions were a joy to behold. They taught me so much; unbeknown to me at that time I would one day have a big project of my own like this but at the time, I just loved going to work.

I met my husband when I returned to England; fell in love and had my children Zach and Lili in quick succession. They are without doubt my biggest achievement and are wonderful little human beings. We set up camp in Cheltenham and spent many happy years as a family. My husband worked away a lot as he was an IT consultant and that brought us many challenges but we faced them the best way we could.

When my daughter was born, we found out that she had some heart problems. Later I was told that the hospital didn't think she was going to make it as she was actually very ill, but at the time we were not told this thank goodness, and Lili continued to thrive and defy the odds. She had a hole in the heart and a rare heart condition called Ebstein's Anomaly which meant she had to be medicated and carefully monitored as she grew. With a sixteen-month-old son and a newborn, I think luckily I was so tired most of the time I didn't have time to even think about how poorly she was, I just had to get on with it.

My first and biggest challenge hit me on a random Friday night in October 2004 when my daughter was three months old. I was house-sitting with my family whilst my mother was away on holiday. Her doorbell rang at 1am and I was met with a police officer holding his cap. He told me to get my husband and told me I needed to sit down. I was then told the news that my brother Matt had been killed on the motorway a couple of hours before. I still remember that day like it was yesterday. I heard wailing – and yes, it was me. Life as I knew it ended for me that night. The Sam I was disappeared and she didn't honestly return for probably three years. Devastated is an understatement. Grief paralysed me and for the next two years and I struggled to function. My mother and I kept going for my children and my brother's son Alex but quite honestly I did not want to be alive. I hated the world and felt very afraid of it. I now knew that nothing was guaranteed and no one was safe. It was and still is, a constant reminder that we all have to make the days count. My husband was amazing and managed somehow to support me but I know how hard that must have been. When you are suffering from grief you become very selfish, as you are incapable of feeling anything but sadness and anger for a long time. The loss ripped me to shreds and I have had to rebuild myself from the ground up; it has made me who I am today but I would do anything to not have had this particular lesson.

To try and cope with this I threw myself into many therapies, and had many illuminating experiences with healers and psychics, all of which slowly helped me to cope. My friends and family held me up and I managed to get through that horrendous first year in some sort of semblance. My father, due to a fallout with my brother, refused to come to his funeral, so I had this anger and disappointment on top to deal with. I had foolishly thought that my father and I would reconnect but it was not meant to be. Talking therapy helped me to deal with my anger and put it to bed. I now feel no anger towards my father, sadness yes, but an understanding that some people aren't meant to be parents.

In 2011 when the children were older, I started to do a little work again and had been doing some marketing for a spa in Cheltenham. The owner of it Emma Whitelaw came to me with an idea as she knew that I was tenacious, creative, and fearless from working with me on her business. She wanted us to form a fashion week for our town, Cheltenham and thought I was the one to get it off the ground. It sparked something in me and I threw myself into it head first. As the project grew in success, so did my confidence and my self- belief. I had always been creative but hadn't done anything for myself for years. I had been a stay at home mum whilst my husband built his career, and now was my time to create something. He agreed, and so I began to work again. But as ever, with a plus comes a negative. As my professional confidence grew, the balance at home shifted. As all working women know and understand, it is very difficult to be everything to everyone and the more I accomplished at work, the less time there was for my home life. I was determined to accomplish my project goals though and had thought my husband was behind me. He wasn't. One Saturday in October my world came crashing down again. My husband announced to me that he didn't love me anymore, that he was leaving me, but would stay through Christmas in our house. That was the first barrel of the shotgun, straight to my chest. *Boom*! I ran straight out of my home, shaking in shock, and crying, to my friend's house. He answered the door, saw me, and crying uncontrollably, I said "Did you know?"

He loaded the gun and the second barrel came, hard. He replied "About X? Yes, I hoped it would end." My husband had been having an affair for six months; when I thought he was out with his friends he had been out with a mum from my kids' school.

Devastated was an understatement. It made no sense to me. I loved him, trusted him, and always thought I would grow old with him. The pain was intense and I completely fell to pieces. I struggled to function through my fashion week, which comprised fourteen events in one week. I wanted to talk things through but he had no interest. He was done. It was totally out of my control. My best friend was gone overnight; the father of my children, and the love of my life. I blamed myself for months, then him, then me again. I honestly thought we would pull through it but it was not meant to be. I probably would not have been able to overcome the trust issues but I would have liked a chance to try, for my children's sake. But that's life I guess.

Male abandonment. Yep, I have been told many a time that in this lifetime, this is to be my karmic lesson. My life had exploded again, I was devastated and shocked and struggled to cope. It took me to a very dark place that I had been once before. Again, I had to face some familiar feelings of abandonment, and somehow rebuild myself once more. It is now nearly three years after that day and I can speak with some experience and thoughts on my life to date.

Self-Love… I think finally I am beginning to feel it. Like everyone I have my good days and my bad days. Anyone who believes that they are amazing every day, well I'm sorry I don't believe it. What do I love about myself, I have to ask, and I guess my answer would be that I am learning from my mistakes every day. After my husband left I did the typical thing, ran around with boys half my age, subscribing to the concept of 'the best way to get over someone is to get under someone else'. I started to feel that actually, I was attractive and worthy of someone's company. I had my heart broken on a monthly basis but with every ending, I got stronger.

Work… This is important for our self-esteem, I can see that now. Children are such a joy and blessing but in caring for them above all else, you cannot help but lose parts of yourself. Even if it is one day a week to keep your skills or passions going – I hate to sound negative but once the children have grown up a little you can really be up Sh*t Creek without a paddle if you haven't got something to throw yourself into. So, be clever girls, keep going at something, you never know how useful it could be later. Do a course from home, a part time college course, volunteer, just keep moving forward, push yourself and keep learning, there are zero downsides to this. Trust me on this one.

When I left LA, I had a phoenix tattoo put onto a certain part of my body, and I do honestly feel that I do keep rising from my own ashes, however corny that sounds. I have my days where I feel insecure but I let those feelings wash over me, and they pass. I know that I am as good as the next person and I guess that's the wisdom of age, right? Or good lighting!

Grief has taught me many things on my road to self-love. It taught me that even when you are at your lowest, it's ok to let others see it and reach out. That being strong is not as important as being honest. Needing help and allowing someone to help you is what life is about. Yes, life is fragile, but actually, the human spirit is not. It is tenacious, optimistic and generous and the bonds, even when seemingly lost through death, are always there in the background if you look hard enough. Trying to hold onto someone when they want to leave is like holding onto sand in your hand, it's impossible. I have finally learned to let go.

Have I failed in my life? I hate the word failure and actually I don't believe there is such a thing. Within each 'failure' there is always something learnt. Therefore, to me it is still about moving forward. I can't claim to be anything like any of these tenacious business people who keep going and going with a drive that is just incredible. All I know is that in my own way I keep moving forward, and with everything that could be construed as a negative in my life, when I look back I can now see the lesson and the reason that it happened. That makes me grateful for it and gives me an understanding of how it has made the person I am today. I honestly 'fail' on many little things daily but I don't worry about them as I prefer to concentrate on the 'big stuff.' I hope that I will have many more opportunities to try things in the next few years, some I will accomplish and some I will not, but I hope to enjoy the 'trying.' Not to try, to me is the biggest failure of all.

Perfect in my imperfections? Absolutely. I cannot honestly imagine anything more boring than a 'perfect' person. Even writing that makes me want to yawn. 'Perfect' just implies that there is no room for improvement and let's face it, everyone needs to continually improve themselves; unless you are Jamie Dorman.

Seriously though, I'd like to be thinner, less wrinkled, more patient, I could write a huge list but it would send you to sleep and I don't want to do that. My fashion project allowed me many opportunities to learn about people, women, self-esteem, and confidence and Jeez it was enlightening. Even the girls with the 'perfect' figures don't see it, but there again, I never saw how gorgeous I was at twenty-five either.

Death does not define me. Does this refer to me dying as God knows what will define me when I'm gone?! Probably my crazy dress sense as my normal clothes have become a 'go to' when people have a fancy-dress party to attend, it's true! No, seriously, death and loss have defined me and made me who I am today, with parts that are still broken but less obvious, and parts that have become more resilient over time. I would do anything to reverse losing my brother, it destroyed me but I built myself up again from the ground. My ex-husband temporarily knocked me down again and certain parts of me will never return but they have been replaced with some inner strength that has been hard won for sure.

I feel that I could do anything now, my independence has been a long time coming and my status as a single mother has allowed me to overcome many of the things I didn't think I could do. My biggest wish for my children is that they will be kind and brave, as to me, that is the best and most powerful combination there is.

As I write this, in August 2017, my future is unknown but no longer am I scared by that. I had to shelve my fashion project temporarily as I felt I needed to get myself back on track before I took it on again. I hope to bring it back if I can. Financially too, I also needed to find my feet as a single working mother. I keep pretty busy. I like not knowing what is around the corner now as I know whatever life throws at me, I will whack it right back even harder.

Biography

Sam Bawden is a creative marketeer, a self-confessed shopaholic of anything vintage or sequinned, a serial consumer of flat whites, and constantly in search of the perfect Mojito. When not working, she's probably talking to her dog Raffa, watching too many American TV shows or dreaming of Jamie Dorman.

www.cheltenhamfashionweek.co.uk
www.winstonswish.org.uk
www.blockclearance.com

Sue Williams

Losing her beloved father, and soon after, her mother, was a catalyst for change for Sue. She had unwittingly become the 'peace-keeper' in her family, the 'good girl,' and became a bit player in her own life – quiet, unassuming, needing to please. Embarking on a journey of self-discovery has led Sue to believe in herself and her abilities, with poetry playing part of the healing process. She now has the confidence to run self-help courses for women.

The Power of Synchronicity

As we neared the end of our Skype conversation, my recently discovered friend remarked: "How refreshing to talk to you. You use the word 'synchronicity' a lot. Not many people I speak to on a day to day basis do that".

To be honest, synchronicities are something that I have only begun to notice and acknowledge for myself very recently. For a substantial number of years, I have had little idea of who I am, how I am feeling or what I want out of life, let alone appreciating any mystical signs popping up before my unseeing eyes!

At the age of fifty, I experienced the first in a chain of events that was to be the catalyst for change. A couple of months after my fiftieth birthday, my father, a quiet, unassuming man, began to experience bloating of his stomach. As was usual, my mother had to push him a number of times before he would visit the doctor. Once he finally did go, he was merely given tablets for water retention.

In August 2009, I embarked on a short visit to a long-standing school friend, now living in Belgium. She was having an informal party at her home to celebrate her birthday, and I was to stay for the weekend. After a pleasant couple of days, enjoying the sunny garden, chatting to people about book clubs, meditation and suchlike, I caught the Eurostar home. My mother and two brothers greeted me with the devastating news that they had been unsure whether to call me or not as dad was in hospital. It had been touch and go whether he would last the weekend.

Hours later, I sat gazing tenderly at my dad, a pale, lonely figure laying in a small, sterile side ward at the General Hospital, a bemused expression on his face. Imperceptibly his head moved to one side. Realising that he wanted to speak to me, I leaned towards him. Straining to hear, I caught the words "I never thought this could happen so quickly."

Possessed of a personality very much like that of my dad – quiet, seeking to fit in, drifting along through life, I understood what he meant. As long as things are on an even keel, in keeping with the daily routine, it feels like nothing will touch you. It is a sense reminiscent of the 'Pollyanna' complex I had maintained since my younger years – everything is sweetness and light, shut out anything that is too difficult to handle.

After a few, short days, my father slipped quietly away in his sleep. In dying he caused no trouble, the same as in life.

A couple of years later, a pertinent Facebook prompt announcing that it was Father's Day, inspired me to commemorate his memory in a poem.

Father's Day

Dad, you popped up unexpectedly on Father's Day,
Seemingly you weren't there, you were locked away,
A faded memory, no longer seen,
Of a person, quiet, sensitive, calm; on the surface, so serene
With an occasional, boyish, sense of humour,
Overlooking you, my own, neglectful, careless bloomer.

Unexpectedly, I espied a memorial rhyme,
On a Facebook page, at exactly the right time,
To remember one whose birthday, 11 November,
Saw peace finally sealed on Armistice day.

Like the widely-commemorated soldier, unknown,
You weren't one to shout out, complain or moan,
A generosity of gentle anonymity routinely held sway.
Unconcerned by antagonistic rumour, life's ups and downs
Zoning out when others yelled, or wore hostile frowns.

Yet in the background, always there,
Amenable, if you had a care.
Not always truly understanding,
Yet, ever calm, loyal and undemanding.

When your time came, suddenly
Slipped away from life's passing scene,
Bewildered by your downward demise; it seemed so mean.
A word that never could have been used to describe you.

Letting Go

Soon after my father passed away, my mother began to experience serious health difficulties. Tests revealed that she had cancer, and a year followed in which I accompanied her on hospital visits, and supported her to move, first into a care home, and finally a nursing home. Rushing to sit with mum after work and at weekends, listening to her tales of care home staff, and witnessing her stoicism, brought me closer to her than had previously seemed possible. Despite the odd bout of criticism, she genuinely appeared to value my support. Nothing summed this up better than my final birthday card from her. My eyes welled with tears as I read her shaky handwriting: "To my lovely daughter Sue xxxxxxxxxxxxxxx." We had finally connected in a meaningful way as mother and daughter.

Doing my best to please my mother was something that was habitually ingrained in me. Although the casual observer might believe that I was an independent, single, career focused woman, the reality couldn't have been further from the truth. For although I went through the motions of working for the Civil Service, mixing with a small group of close knit friends, and appearing placid and accepting of life, the truth was that I was following my father's pattern of zoning out. Inside my mind was constantly over thinking and over analysing everything, particularly what was wrong with me. Although I lived at a distance from my mother, it was like I carried her demands and admonitions with me everywhere in my thoughts. I also experienced life as if one step removed; for example, rather than appreciate them for myself, whenever I looked at flowers my only thought would be "mum would love these."

You might be wondering how a fifty-one-year-old woman could become so tied up with her mother. Looking back, as a quiet, sensitive child, this was all too easy. Unconsciously, I would pick up on the thoughts and feelings my mother was experiencing, and internalise them. I had a desire to please, and the only way that I knew how to do that was to keep the peace. So, whenever my mother launched into a critical string of words, or made demands, I would retreat inside myself until the thunderstorm subsided. Similarly, when I recognised that I did no good at all in intervening in boisterous arguments between my two brothers, I took a back seat. The positive aspects of being the 'peace keeper' rebounded on me, and as the years passed, I increasingly became a bit part player in my own life.

In my mid to late forties, I found myself struggling to exert myself at work. Difficult situations with a line manager and a strong-minded colleague took their toll. It seemed like I was constantly swimming through treacle, flailing around trying to get the upper hand. Eventually, after one particularly anxious, long drawn out battle of wills with a work colleague, I took positive action. I applied successfully for a promotion, which involved a change of geographical area. I moved nearer to my mother, who had recently suffered a stroke, allowing me to take her out for drives in the countryside she loved. This was the main way I had of pleasing her.

After a stressful re-organisation lasting nine months, during which time I again experienced tensions with demands from my line manager, the relentless cycle of restructuring followed a brief period of rewarding work. I allowed myself to be increasingly side-lined by acquiescing to management decisions to take roles that neither inspired nor motivated me. Of course, it would never have entered my mind to say 'no' to a move, when to say 'yes' meant that I was keeping the peace, and 'being the good girl'.

Finally, during a time when much of the working day consisted of trying to look busy, whilst management played political infighting, I was offered the opportunity of early retirement! Unlike some colleagues, anxious to keep their jobs, saying yes seemed a 'no brainer' to me. The opportunity of a small pension and a new start away from deadening routine appealed greatly.

No sooner had the decision been made, than news came that the trial drug my mum had been taking, for which we had high hopes, had made no impact. Mum only had weeks to live. Fortuitously, leaving work enabled me to spend ample time with her in her final days.

Mum was a very intelligent, independent minded and creative person. She was, I now realise, also frustrated and unfulfilled. As I sat with her in her final few months, I understood some of the challenges she had faced in life. Career minded, yet with traditional beliefs, she had been forced to give up work once she became pregnant with my elder brother. But more than that, from snippets of conversation, I realised that she had carried unspoken guilt within her throughout her life. She had an elder brother who died at around the age of four or five, before mum was born. In those days, it was not the done thing to talk about such things or dwell on them. Her parents bottled up their grief inside.

On one of my dutiful visits, mum told me that, as a young girl, she had stumbled across her unknown brother's things whilst exploring the depths of an old, walnut coloured wardrobe in her father's bedroom. My grandfather, a bluff, well-built man, had come in, found her, and shouted at her that she was never to go in there again. Scared to death of her father, mum vowed that she would marry a man who was nothing like him.

Gradually, I saw how this self-fulfilling prophecy had unfolded. My father was one of the meekest, mildest men I knew. However, the imbalance in their personalities had allowed mum's more controlling, dominant side to come to the fore, in compensation for dad's easy-going persona. The rest of the family bore the brunt of this, and it seemed we were never good enough. It was as if in seeking to avoid a man like my grandfather, mum had herself, unwittingly taken on his more controlling characteristics.

Mum carried a lot of misplaced guilt, feeling that she could never make up for the disappointment of not having been born a boy – a replacement for the son who died so young. I, in turn grew up lacking a strong father figure, my sensitive nature internalising by osmosis the pain my mum didn't know how to express.

This, combined with my desperation to please mum, and an inability to feel my own emotions meant I tended to see everything through her eyes. Mum also liked to live her imaginary life through me, telling me that I should go to teach in Canada, or run a magazine, without recognising what a big leap this would have been, even if I had clarity to know these things were what I even wanted. I felt unable to connect meaningfully with any passion for a career myself.

Leaving a legacy.

It is important to acknowledge that my mother did the best she could in the circumstances in which she found herself. In recognising that, I see that I am on an evolving journey to fulfil my own purpose on this earth, and heal the family line.

Shine For Me

As you remember me this day,
Let sweetness blend with sorrow,
You are my gift,
Left on this earth,
To create a brighter tomorrow.
And, as you ever blossom and grow,
My legacy lives on,
So be my light,
Within this world,
Through you, still brightly shone.

New Beginnings.

Suddenly, in late October 2010, I faced the fact that, without a job or parents I had lost all of the stable features in my life. It dawned on me that I had absolutely no idea about who I was or what I wanted to do with my life! However, I had vast amounts of time stretching before me, and a more substantial amount of dispensable money than ever before, having the luxury of both a lump sum from work and money inherited from my parents.

A chance email from a coaching school triggered a journey of self-discovery that would involve undertaking many courses, healings and experiences.

Initially, I found myself trying to replace work, becoming too focused on the idea of starting a business and striving to find an elusive niche. I was susceptible to the practised sales techniques of some marketers and signed up for expensive courses that in many cases ended up repeating the same messages again and again – find a niche, make six figures. I also became powerfully aware of the need to heal the locked away emotions that I had avoided for so long, and undertook training in Neuro-Linguistic Programming (NLP), reiki, spiritual coaching, angel card reading, and explored various healing modalities. Answers to questions such as 'What is your big why?' 'What are your passions?' 'What did you enjoy doing in your childhood?' remained stubbornly elusive. I remembered little of my childhood, or even much of my schooling. However, I clearly remembered being actively engaged in writing an essay in answer to an exam question: 'What is the difference between portraiture and photography?'. Although I only possessed an Instamatic camera to snap pictures, and struggled to produce anything recognisable in art class, this topic struck a surprising chord. It was like a seed was planted in fertile ground as I explored the different perspectives.

Resisting Writing.

As time passed, some healers encouraged me to write. However, I remained resistant, until I met a very enthusiastic coach. My working relationship with this coach commenced with a clear synchronicity. Having listened to her engaging talk at a networking event, I felt a strong pull to work with her. Yet, I had decided not to spend further money on courses. Towards the end of the meeting, I wrestled internally, trying to stand firm. After a few minutes, I turned my head, to find that the coach and I were the only two people left in the room. With an electric spark of recognition, I knew then that we were meant to work together!

This enthusiastic coach helped me to recognise my tendency to flat-line my emotions. One day, she sent me an email bubbling over with excitement for a new notion she had for me. When we spoke, my sense of anticipation turned to deflation, as she revealed her amazing suggestion was that I should write morning pages. Writing again! However, as she was so thrilled with this proposal, I didn't have the heart to refuse.

Dutifully, I agreed to write for half an hour each morning about anything and everything that came into my head. Imagine my surprise, when after about ten days of this practice, my writing began to emerge in rhyme. It wouldn't necessarily make sense, but it would rhyme!

Subsequently, an opportunity arose to produce a book for an event my coach planned to run, called: 'Believe in Your Dreams, Your Legacy, Your Power'. Feeling motivated by this prospect, I sat down at my computer one morning, and to my great surprise a poem flowed as my fingers tapped gently on the keys. In front of me emerged a clarion call to believe in myself!

Believe!

Stand up, stand up! Be bold, be strong.
Your talent, on a world stage, truly does belong.
You are a beacon, shining bright,
Birthed to emerge, grow, and shine your inner light!

It is a crime to leave talent, dusty on rickety, hidden shelves,
Set out your stall; allow true expression of your amazing inner selves.
Surely, you will experience some discomfort as you stretch,
Far better than staying a self-defeating, self-pitying little wretch?
Rather, as you experience movement, create life-changing shifts,
You will, newly emboldened, dare to share your gifts!

Life is truly meant for us to live; by our own expression, give
To those, like us, who have sometimes been
Squashed, ignored, or diligently working; self-effacing, behind a screen
Of uniformity; water poured on burning fire,
Quashed down, made damp squib of all passion and desire.

And, as others bask in your new golden glow,
It helps for them, also to know,
That they have their own miracles to perform,
Whether on a stage, or as more often is the norm,
In their own families and communities, through their daily life and deeds.
Do great work; sow and nurture the seeds
Of positivity, purposefulness and joy,
With which we all entered this world to buoy
Up ourselves and others, to manifest the birth-right of our mothers,
As we mix with friends, many others, who enter into life's stratosphere.
All add dark and shade, maybe cause us to shed a tear,
Perhaps of joy or sometimes pain,
So, ultimately, of our own truth, understanding we gain.

Right here and now, we need to show,
Through heartfelt determination, strength of courage,
We all have the power to foster our own abilities, to grow;

> Achieve our birth-right to succeed; root out the dreaded weed
> That with stranglehold choked down our well-intentioned schemes,
> Left us struggling with dashed hopes, and broken, once beautiful dreams.
> Meaning-full, join us to create,
> An interwoven, brilliant picture with which all can relate!
> As one voice, stand up and state:
> "We are here to live mindfully in this life,
>
> We choose creativity, positive intent over unrewarding strife
> And as we choose to change how we ourselves perceive,
> In our own dreams, our legacy, our power, we truly believe!"

Sadly, the event reduced in scale and a book was no longer needed. I saved the poem on my computer, and left it hidden away in a forgotten folder.

Following the bread crumbs.

Oddly, poetry increasingly appeared in subtle ways in my life. I would hear it mentioned on TV or in newspapers or magazines. I had that curious, tingly sensation of 'knowing' that I was being given little signs or nudges, but I was not sure why. Silently, I determined to follow the trail of breadcrumbs.

In May 2012, I felt optimistic as I queued to embark on a cruise ship, ready to explore the Mediterranean. Glancing at a rack containing various free publications, I selected a copy of a popular women's magazine. Having returned to my place, an intangible impulse caused me to turn again to look at the rack. Suddenly, I espied a writer's magazine I had previously missed. Returning to the shelves, I picked it up. "I wonder whether there is anything about poetry in it," I mused. Intriguingly, as I flicked through the glossy pages, I uncovered an article about a course on writing poetry as therapy. Stunned, I discovered it was to be delivered in Falmouth, where, coincidently, a close friend had only recently moved. It felt like this was meant to be, and I immediately resolved to go.

The course provided a very gentle, non-judgemental introduction to the power of poetry; a great escape route for expressing the hidden joys, sadness, worries or torments that might not otherwise surface. We were asked not to analyse the perceived quality of each other's writing, which made it easier to share aloud. I began to feel more positive about pursuing my poetry. I also took to sharing poems in a safe, closed women's group of which I was a member on social media, and valued the supportive comments I received.

Soon afterwards, I attended a workshop for women held by Tribal Truth. As I waited to be paired up with one of the other women for an informal coaching arrangement, I sensed that I would be linked to a coach who was reinventing herself as a photographer. Sure enough, we were placed together!

Subtle, insistent signs continued; each one unconsciously registered and logged. Incongruously, as I returned to relax in my hotel room after training, a poet was the subject of a detective drama. Gradually, I realised I was being nudged away from coaching and niches, and towards poetry.

During a 'buddy' session with the would-be photographer, I volunteered to have a photo session, to help her build a portfolio in preparation for her new career. Nervously, I waited to see the resulting pictures. I did a double take as I first glanced at one of the pictures, I almost didn't recognise the beaming portrait that gazed back at me! I felt as if the picture captured a shining, inner essence of my best self.

"Sue, stand up, stand up!"

On browsing the files in my laptop, I stumbled across the 'Believe'! poem which I had so carelessly cast aside months earlier.

Gazing at the first line of my poem the words: 'Stand up, stand up! Be bold, be strong,' it suddenly became blindingly obvious – this poem was an urgent message to me, I needed to follow my first inclination and publish a book.

I decided to treat this as a project, to see whether I could do it. After all of the networking and training that I had been doing, surely, I had enough contacts willing to contribute their inspirational stories and poems. Although it hit a few sticky moments, the book was completed, and that wonderful photograph took pride of place next to my author profile on the back cover.

In May 2013, I held an event to launch the book. I felt proud to stand up and tell my story, surrounded by people who believed in me enough to share their own stories and poems in the book. The buzz of chatter and connection was amazing, and an acknowledgement of the power of following my intuition. That intuition recently led me to a post on Facebook by an inspirational woman looking to produce this book.

Continuing the journey.

I still see myself very much as a work in progress. I continue to experience situations in which I find it difficult to assert myself or to know what my own boundaries are. I am learning to explore the creative side of myself, and to let go of the past. To hear my new friend acknowledge the extent to which I talk about synchronicity underlines how far I have travelled on my journey to self- belief. I continue to write poetry as part of the healing process.

Taking note of the signs, I will publish my first collection in 2017. Today, there are more opportunities than ever to explore and express our creativity. How curious that an innocuous essay question written at the age of eighteen still inspires me today. I believe that, as Women of Spirit, collaboration is a key way forward, and I am proud to be following my intuition to work with other spirited and creative women to uncover the power of self-belief and self- expression.

Biography

Sue took early retirement from the Civil Service at the age of fifty-one, where she developed career information, advice and guidance services for adults. Embarking on a journey of self-discovery and healing, led her to the 'morning pages', a technique for unlocking creative self-expression.

Sue collated and published two collections of true life stories on the topic of self- belief, and has also developed a set of colourful and inspiring 'Believe' oracle cards and an associated App which won a Gold award in the 2017 Janey Loves awards.

In September 2016 Sue ran her first event for women: 'Your Signature Success Story' and in 2017 published her first book of poetry, *I Am Unique*. She is currently developing further services for women aged fifty plus to help them to define success in their own terms.

www.sue-williams.com

Di Lofting

Born in wartime, Dawn's childhood and family life was torn apart when her beloved older sister died. An emotionally bereft childhood didn't prevent Di from embarking upon an adventurous career as a nurse, ultimately pioneering new pelvic floor exercises and therapies, enabling patients to claim back their lives. Sadly, Di passed away shortly after I photographed her holding her book for the first time – but through both N*ever Say Di* and *Women of Spirit*, her spirit and humour live on.

Written by Sue Kelso Ryan, ghostwriter of her book *Never say Di*

Di Lofting was never one to let life's hurdles get in the way; on the contrary, she was determined to grab every opportunity. She was born in wartime, to a mother who was unable to offer her love and so she endured a difficult childhood, clinging to her older sister Wendy for affection and guidance. While still very young, she was sent away to boarding school and just a few years later Di's world was rocked when Wendy died tragically. Her parents separated and her father withdrew in his grief, leaving Di to cope alone, both emotionally and practically. But she didn't let these events define or limit her. Di dragged herself up by her bootlaces, determined to 'go for it' and make the most of life.

> Really one should write memoirs when one is younger – we'd recall the details more clearly that way. The trouble is, I was far too busy living my life to take notes. You might think you can spot a plan in the things I have done, a well thought-out route from A to T (we're not quite at Z yet) with carefully scheduled stops along the way. If you can, you're doing better than me. There was no plan, you see.
>
> Diane Lofting, 2016

It was her practical nature that made Di's decision to become a nurse an obvious one – she needed a roof over her head and that's what nursing would provide. She had already demonstrated her caring nature in looking after her devastated father – deserted by his wife and broken-hearted about the death of his daughter. Di was grief-stricken too but she carried on and made the best of the opportunities around her. Ever the adventurer, she seized on the opportunity to visit Canada after qualifying, intending to use her nursing skills abroad. She roped in four of her many friends and headed for Edmonton, where she was immediately plunged into a world of intrigue – she became a spy! Unable to tell her friends about her involvement with the Canadian drug squad, Di proved her resourcefulness and the spirited young woman helped to apprehend the culprit, while serenely continuing her regular nursing duties.

Aside from her career as a nurse, Di enjoyed adventures such as skiing and climbing, travelling and exploring whenever she could. Nursing is a flexible career and she was able to visit New Zealand, which she explored on her beloved Vespa, Blossom, despite breaking her arm. She even accidentally opened a new road; she was the first person to motor down it and was greeted by a reception committee of journalists and important locals at the far end. In Australia, where Blossom was traded for a Morris Minor, Di set off again, discovering the outback and venturing up the east coast, where she fell in love with an island in the Whitsundays but not with the predatory males whose attentions she escaped. Relating her adventures in her book, Never Say Di, she often said, "I shouldn't have been there!" as she remembered the scrapes she got into and the perils she narrowly avoided. It was unusual for a young woman to travel alone in such remote areas but, as she put it, 'I survived!'

Having experienced nursing in New Zealand and Australia, Di returned to her career in the UK but she was still restless and soon signed up for Voluntary Service Overseas work in Tanzania. Di was posted to a city hospital that received patients from many backgrounds and tribes, in fairly primitive conditions. She was responsible for teaching nursing staff and she was drawn to working with children afflicted by polio, which was still rife there in the 1960's. She even tried to adopt a young polio patient but the authorities refused her permission and she never learnt what became of young Anna.

Meeting Di, the first thing that you noticed was her stubborn refusal to take life seriously and the twinkle in her eye indicated that she was always ready for a laugh and some fun. If there was humour in a situation, Di would find it, especially if the joke was on her. She told many stories about situations that she got into that would have been too much for others to cope with – facing down wild animals or angry matrons among them. This strength of character served her well but also led her to a problem-solving attitude – she refused to accept that things had to be the way they always had been and couldn't be changed.

One of the biggest effects Di had on the nursing profession and on the patients in her care came when, as a nursing manager in Bath, she noticed that much of her nursing budget was being spent on products to help those suffering from incontinence. Although her intention was to save the NHS money, the effect was to empower patients (both male and female). By pioneering the new pelvic floor exercises and other therapies,

Di helped these patients to claim back their lives, whether that was a ballroom dancing hobby or the ability to look after their family. Not a sexy achievement, as Di was the first to admit, but nevertheless it made her a hero in many people's eyes.

Di was recognised for her nursing work by the Royal College of Nursing. Much more importantly, she was a much-loved wife, stepmother and friend with a host of activities and hobbies that kept her very busy. She introduced her step-grandsons to skiing and it was during short trips on ski lifts that she refined her story-telling abilities, keeping the boys amused with anecdotes about her past. She would tell them about the day she decided it was more efficient to put all the patients' false teeth in the same bowl at once in order to wash them; only realising her error when it was time to give them back and she didn't know which teeth belonged to which patient.

One of Di's hobbies was photography and she not only recorded her many overseas trips and holidays in the UK, she also volunteered her services as photographer for her golf club in Bath. Golf was something she took up for the social life and she formed many lasting friendships. Though her handicap didn't improve as quickly as she would have liked, golf appealed to her competitive spirit. It could be said that conquering handicaps was something at which Di was a past master – the most monstrous of these for her was the overwhelming disability of dyslexia. She felt very keenly her lack of academic achievement, comparing herself to her clever sister Wendy and still, years later, recalling the humiliation of having teachers mock her inability to read and write fluently.

And so, Di being Di, she decided that she would write a book. Of course she did. She advertised for, and found, a ghostwriter and set about recording her adventures to encourage others in the belief that they can still achieve, despite dyslexia. There was a trigger for writing the book and sadly it was Di's diagnosis with what proved to be terminal cancer. Again, she was determined that the book would get written while she was still able to work on the project and that it would act as an inspiration and encouragement to others with serious illness or other obstacles in their path to happiness. The title, *Never Say Di*, was chosen very deliberately, to reflect Di's stubborn attitude and that twinkle in her eye. She had even picked out the principal actors for 'her' film; Meryl Streep to play Di and

Pierce Brosnan to take the lead as her beloved husband, Ray.

To her great joy, Di was able to hold the completed book in one hand and a glass of champagne in the other when Susie and her ghostwriter, Sue Kelso Ryan, took it to her. Sadly, she died a few weeks later and didn't hear of the 5- star reviews the book has received:

> A little gem. Don't read unless you want to fall in love with Di. Di says she's been brought up fearless and you won't be sorry she was. Beside the adventures, you'll discover the most loveable, positive and inspiring lady.

Never Say Di – The Ordinary Tale Of An Extraordinary Woman, by Diane Lofting, as told to Sue Kelso Ryan is available as an e-book from Amazon or as a softcover book from Blurb.com. See www.suekelsoryan.co.uk for details and links to purchase. All proceeds from the sale of *Never Say Di* go to Dorothy House Hospice Care in Bath, whose staff provided superb care to Di Lofting in her final weeks.

www.dorothyhouse.org.uk

Alice and Lucy Steels

These two beautiful young women are the daughters of my dearest friend Sally, and I've known them all their lives. We lost our darling Sally to pancreatic cancer in 2015, a battle she fought with true dignity and love, for she was one of the most loving people I've known. Reading the girls' wise words will fill you with hope – the beauty within never dies, it lives on. Sally agreed to appear in my book but we never got around to telling her story, so I am truly thankful to her daughters for their reflections. Darling Sally, you are much missed, and always loved.

OUR DARLING MUMMY, SALLY GAYLE WILLIAMS, was the heroine of our lives. Sweet, gentle to all and funny – we loved her dearly and continue to carry the memory of her essence and legacy of love in our hearts. Sally was known in her twenties as a red head Yorkshire lass who was raised in the very regal 'The Mount', York, and later she was a sweetheart who loved city life in London with a great friend whom she fondly called 'Delly'; also known as Adele. Her long red hair and bohemian look captured the attention of many during her younger years, and it was the essence of her kindness that captured the heart of many in her later years.

Mum and Susie met in 1984 at a cocktail party organised by our father for the military in Aldershot; they instantly became the greatest of friends and never, ever had a cross word.

It was in London that she met our father in the eighties and our lives began there – '87 and '91, to be precise! During this marriage she made fond memories and made two new sisters with whom she shared a sense of style. She found a new mother – very different to her own – who loved her and found her interesting. Sadly, work and family tensions meant that the marriage didn't work out, and our parents divorced when we were young. In honesty, the following twenty or so years were a mixture for Mum which held a set of their own hardships in life and subsequent marriages. Life wasn't especially easy or happy, particularly after two divorces, but one thing that we remember with joy is that she never stopped smiling, and she never stopped loving. Her smile and care was like a spoon full of medicine to us in itself.

Fast forward to 2015 and we can hardly believe that we were kissing goodbye to our Mum, after a gruelling eighteen month battle with pancreatic cancer. A tragedy, yes but a tale interwoven with great hope. For those who have lost a loved one you may understand some of the things we are about to describe, as loss of some kind is something we have all been through. It is a journey of the heart so unique and tender to every person affected by the loss – an intricate web of sorrow, celebration, memories and heartache – a tragedy that we believe only someone infinitely greater than us has all of the answers to.

Losing our Mum to cancer in our twenties and witnessing the process of her illness was excruciating. But precious gems of intimate moments with the one who brought us into the world, throughout her treatment, have helped to soothe the grief over the years. This recent time has been one of adapting to existing relationships with a new dynamic, without our queen, and with the chance to reminisce of blessed times with gratitude for ever having them at all with a mother who loved us. Strangely enough, treasuring times together was always something we wanted to do as a family, perhaps because deep down somewhere we knew the fragility of life and that things of this life may not last forever.

Here Lucy reflects a little further on her own experience of the difficult time and describes what brought peace in the storm…

I remember the day she was diagnosed. 27th August 2013. I was in the office and it was a white noise moment. A moment of terror. My heart froze and through the fuzz I heard a colleague asking if she could order me a taxi to the hospital. I decided to drive, braving the fifteen mile journey up to the hospital where Mum had received the news. I arrived in her ward and remember seeing the sadness on her sweet face, and her bright orange hair which she had home- dyed for a number of years. It broke my heart. I climbed into her hospital bed with her and cuddled up to watch a programme on the little television, nestling into her chest like a little babe, wondering what the future held. We tried to be as normal as we could and talked about girly things as usual.

Alice, too, would drive miles from London so we could be together at home, and while it was a stressful time all round, simply being together at the end of it all was enough.

So, where life had seemed to be heading one way for my sister and me, with careers, friendships and the like, there was now a drastic U-turn and we were on an unknown road together as a family. But there was great hope. The, Great Hope. At the bottom of this deep, ugly, marshy valley I found Jesus Christ; my friend, the tangible light at the end of the tunnel, and the lover of my soul. I had come to the end of myself and He had come to my rescue.

Encountering God's love and peace in my heart was an indescribable experience as I broke down on the bathroom floor on Christmas Eve, asking Him to forgive me for my broken ways. It was (and is) an eternal love, joy, strength, and comfort which has never left the core of my being.

So, here we were on the road to redemption after some years of fractured family reality. Months of crying and laughing, planning parties, midnight Marmite-on-toast, trying on wigs for chemo – Mum, not us! And bravery on all sides. Finding treasure in each day and at every family meal. Exploring our souls, our pasts, our hopes and our dreams for the future. And excitingly, a new-found faith in God, our Creator.

Like most Mum's, ours was a 'do-er'. She always did well with what she put her hand to – cooking, sewing, designing and organising. She was also a beauty queen; a graduate of the Lucy Clayton modelling school and musically gifted in guitar and piano. She loved the 'old days' of the fashionable sixties and seventies, and the 'new days' of family and exploring Christian life. Yes, there were bad decisions made along the way in her life which profoundly affected our lives and wounded us deeply, but through her sickness we were able to confront these difficult things of the past and move forward into new pastures. That's real redemption and true love – only such perfection can come from a Heavenly Father who knows us intimately. The One who was in our past, who sees our present, and is to come in the future.

Fast-forward eighteen months and we say goodbye to our best friend, weeping over her tiny, broken frame as she fights for her life. I say I'm sorry for any areas where I may have hurt her and even in all of her delusion from the morphine, she was able to raise her arms around my neck and say "my baby, my baby" and kiss me so softly on the cheek. A mother's love really is relentless. An unbreakable, unconditional, unwavering love. I'm eternally grateful for that moment, a moment of forgiveness so precious. An exchange of the heart between a mother and a daughter.

A sad story yes, but certainly not the end of the tale. My fairytale goes on – Divine Romance in God – and the legacy of Sally (Porter) Williams lives on in me and my precious sister.

We will forever grieve the physical presence of Mum, but find peace in knowing that death was never a part of God's plan. I'm happier. I am alive to the realities and mysteries of my faith. My Spirit is awakened to the Truth, and my soul on a journey of renewal. How wonderful a gift it is to be journeying on this road called life.

> So, we fix our eyes not on what is seen, but on what is unseen, since what is seen is temporary, but what is unseen is eternal.
>
> 2 Corinthians

While I understand that not all people have had the same spiritual experience or awakening in the same way I have, I hope that this may bring hope to others who are searching. In 2017, life has brought Alice and me engagements to the loves of our lives for which we are so thankful, and so excited for what's next in store – and for married life!

Biographies

Alice lives in London with her fiancé, working for the past five years for a Seattle based technical company. After losing her mother, Alice has a new perspective on life, sees it as an adventure, and continues to make the most of it. She marries her best friend next year and knows that her mother will be there in spirit and forever in her heart. She looks forward to becoming a mother herself and showing her babies the most perfect kind of love that her mother gave her.

Lucy lives and works in London as a personal assistant. Her passion is to volunteer with women who have been through human trafficking and prostitution, listening to their stories. Lucy enjoys writing, travelling and climbing mountains with her sister when possible! Being outdoors – rain or shine, city or countryside – is Lucy's favourite place to be!

www.pcrf.org.uk

Author's Note

Putting together this book has been a fascinating journey for me, the road not without its rocky patches along the way. The idea for 'Women of Spirit' first came about for a college project in 2004, when I was a new ('mature') student embarking on a photography degree. Choosing one of the set phrases 'do not pass me by', I set out to find unsung heroines, those whose stories had not yet been told. Where to find such women? Almost immediately I realised that all I had to do was listen, for they were all around me.

Each woman I interviewed reached deep into herself to share her experiences; some more traumatic than others but each story deserves to be told. Modesty is a quality shared by each woman, and their generosity of spirit has been heart-warming. I hope you will feel this too. It was a privilege to be allowed more than just a glimpse into what makes these women tick, and my thanks goes to each one of them.

This book is a celebration of the lives of these women, of their quiet strength and positive attitude. I hope their stories will be an inspiration to those of you who may be facing your own, similar challenges – you are not alone.

So here we are, at the beginning of the Women of Spirit movement. It seems apt to be embarking upon this now, with next year being the 100th anniversary of the Women's Suffragette Movement in the UK. Women fought hard for, and won the right to vote with a Parliamentary Act of 1918, but it took another decade for women to gain equal terms to men to vote. Amazingly, women could still not become police officers, jurors, or lawyers; could not graduate from Oxford or Cambridge – and most disturbingly, rape in marriage was not a crime.

We've come a long way, but with issues such as the startling gender pay gaps in large corporations and the false 'flawless perfection' with which we are surrounded and to which we cannot possibly aspire, clearly there is still a long way to go.

So this book, my first publication, is intended to be the first of many such volumes, for by working together we can achieve so much more.

Mission Statement

To inspire and empower women to develop a healthy sense of self and to know their true worth.

Vision Statement

For women to lead a life full of confidence and strong self-worth, a world in which we inspire each other towards self-empowerment.

If You Enjoyed…

If you found this book worthwhile, please help us spread the word by popping onto Amazon.co.uk and writing a review. Thank you!

You are also very welcome to join our wonderful community on Facebook and Instagram – links via our website www.womenofspirit.co.uk.

www.ingramcontent.com/pod-product-compliance
Lightning Source LLC
Chambersburg PA
CBHW042114100526
44587CB00025B/4044